Put PEAK in your WEEK

Copyright © 1985
Marvin Phillips
**No part of this book may be
reproduced in any form without
written permission from Author.**

Put PEAK in Your WEEK

"Introduction by: Dr. Norman Vincent Peale"

Marvin Phillips

HOWARD BOOK HOUSE

3117 North 7th
West Monroe, Louisiana 71291

DEDICATION

to
the 400 members
of my "Peak of
the Week" class.

Meeting with you
has been the "Peak"
of my week for the
last three years!

IN APPRECIATION

No one is able to do anything really worthwhile without the help of many others. I have many to thank, this time. Among them:

I thank good friends in professional speaking who have been mentors to me. Especially Dr. Norman Vincent Peale, Zig Ziglar and Jim Cathcart. Their advice and suggestions about my speaking career have been invaluable.

I thank the Elders of the Garnett Church of Christ, where I have served as minister since 1970. They believe in me, and further believe the work I do in writing and professional speaking is as effective as my days in the office!

I thank the National Speakers Association. I've been a member for a number of years, and their monthly newsletter, tape-of-the month program, and annual conventions have been so helpful to me in speaking and writing.

I thank our daughter, Tammy Bresee and Myrna Baldridge, my secretary who faithfully and lovingly typed the manuscript for this book.

I thank my wife of thirty-two years, Dot, for continued love and loyalty. She is my greatest asset and my continued inspiration.

Last of all, I thank my God, for making all of us in His image, and designing us to "Fly on wings as eagles" (Isa. 40:31).

Dear Marvin,

I feel as though I know you because I have heard you speak and have listened to a lot of your tapes. I just finished your book "You Can't Fly to Heaven in a Straight Line." Now this is not flattery but praise. WOW! What a great encouraging book!

I am a preacher's wife and mother of 5—ages 17, 15, 14, 11 and 3. I try to "stay up" but get discouraged at times. Your book was a real blessing for me. *Please write us another one*—your enthusiasm is catching. My husband probably won't recognize me when we eat lunch together. So he will probably want to thank you also.

>Enjoyed and drank up every word of your book.
>Thanks so much,
>
>Christian Love,
>
>
>Cindy Hall

PREFACE

AN IDEA THAT CAUGHT FIRE!

You've watched telephone poles, haven't you!? You've noticed how the line between them drops to its lowest point in the middle, and angles up to the pole on each end. Well that's the way most peoples' lives go during the week. And that would make "Wednesday" the lowest point in the week. Wednesday isn't Monday (coming in from a refreshing weekend); and it isn't Friday (looking forward to a day off). It lies there for many, like the power line at it's "lowest point"!

Now I wear several hats. I speak at positive thinking rallies around the country with some of the top name speakers in America. And I am minister for the Garnett Church of Christ, one of the largest and most positive churches in the nation. It was in this latter role, where I teach a Wednesday night adult Bible class, that this "Peak" idea was formed!

An informal rap one night with my class of about 150, confirmed this business of the "Wednesday Blahs"! I said, "What would PEAK your week on a Wednesday?" Replies came in such as, "we need a boost", "we need someone to believe in us"; "we need some encouragement"; "something to look forward to"! We discussed every detail of such a class, and came up with the format I've used for over two years now.

Now I normally try lots of new ideas. But to keep from wearing them out, I usually do them for only 13 weeks (one quarter). But this one hit a need; it serviced a hurt. The class grew from 150 to over 400. It is a "standing room only" situation Wednesday after Wednesday. I know we're on to something, therefore, we will likely do the "PEAK OF THE WEEK CLASS" from now on.

Every class is a positive, lively, fast-moving experience. I promise a "lift" to all who come! You can count on Wednesday night being "just what you need" to believe in yourself again, to be drawn closer to God and each other;

to get a greater kick out of living!

In addition to the lessons, the informal format of the class lends to the entire experience of the hour long session.

We start with the "hugger/huggee" line! Psychologists, doctors and even the Bible urges us to be "kindly affectioned one to another with brotherly love." The value of touch is an established fact! I never embarrass my class by asking everyone to "hug the one on the right, and the one on the left." Instead, I ask for volunteer "huggers" to come up and stand beside me. Usually six or eight men and women will join me in the hugging line. Then I give the entire audience two minutes to come through the hugging line. It is a marvelous experience both for those in the line, and for the ones who sit in the audience. They seem to enjoy it too! There must be value in watching others hug!

We have a class song which has the line, "Bind us together, Lord, with chains that cannot be broken." We join hands all across the room for the song, and then I have them repeat after me at the top of their voices:

> "I'm made in God's Image!
> I can choose my attitude!
> I choose to feel great!"

We have prayer, and the class begins.

Several undeniable proofs convince me, that we're on the right track with this class. One is the obvious doubling in attendance. Another is that members more enthusiastically bring visitors to that class than any other activity we have. The word spreads to others needing that "weekly boost"! People with hurting marriages have come, and along with some private counseling, have found happiness together again. Many have become more interested in spiritual matters, and were soon taught and became Christians.

This book is the result of many requests to get into print these weekly sessions that we all enjoy. It is a labor of love! The class is my "family within the family"!

I hope this book, "PEAKS" your week! Better yet, I hope it "PEAKS YOUR LIFE"! And if it does, I am more than rewarded for the time and effort herein spent!

Table of Contents

Preface	*An Idea That Caught Fire*............	9
Chapter 1	*Getting the Most Out of Life*........	13
Chapter 2	*The Road to Anywhere!*...............	17
Chapter 3	*Teaching Pelicans How to Fish!*..	23
Chapter 4	*Cowboys Don't Walk Home!*........	29
Chapter 5	*Three Dimensional Love!*............	35
Chapter 6	*A Year of Octobers!*...................	41
Chapter 7	*Don't Knock Re-runs!*.................	45
Chapter 8	*How to be "Up" When You're "Down"!*...............	49
Chapter 9	*Never Order Vanilla!*..................	53
Chapter 10	*No One Wants A Pet Buzzard!*...	57
Chapter 11	*Fool Things I've Done*................	63
Chapter 12	*You're Not Old Til You're Old!*..	69
Chapter 13	*Your Beautiful Body!*..................	75
Chapter 14	*I Never Knew You Liked Piña Coladas*............................	81
Chapter 15	*Clouds!*..	85
Chapter 16	*Your Face After Forty Is Your Own Fault!*.......................	89
Chapter 17	*The Masks We Wear!*.................	95
Chapter 18	*Who Touched Me?*.......................	101
Chapter 19	*The Day Everything Went Wrong*	107
Chapter 20	*Lovers Live Longer*.....................	113
Chapter 21	*The Persimmon Secret!*...............	119
Chapter 22	*Who Wrote the Book on "Normal"?*...................................	123
Chapter 23	*Looking At Life Through Proper Perspectacles!*............................	129
Chapter 24	*Seeds Come Before Flowers!*.......	135
Chapter 25	*Quality Control!*.........................	141

FOREWORD

"Put Peak in Your Week!" is one of the most interesting, really motivating, "motivational" books I've read in many a day. It's good! Real good!

If you're down, this book will lift you up. If you're discouraged read "Put Peak in Your Week!" and you'll be insulated with a new shot of courage. The book is written to stimulate fresh attitudes that are highly positive in nature. I am sure that, as you read and practice Marvin Phillips' ideas, you will get a dynamic new lease on life. You will have not only a peak in your week, but perhaps a highpeak in your total life. The book content, when absorbed and assimilated is designed to give any reader a new faith that will wipe out those lows that creep in upon us now and then.

The book is written in a delightfully readable style just as if Dr. Phillips were talking with you at a coffee break. He has a human and genuinely stimulating personality. And besides, he is a loving, caring man. In the book he comes through as a person who likes you and believes in you. And Marvin is just like that. I know, for I have spoken on the same platform with him at not a few meetings across the country. He inspires people. He is experienced and wise and therefore a good counselor and competent guide.

"Put Peak in Your Week!" by Marvin Phillips is a fine book for reading and practicing creative principles that will perk up your life and put a permanent high peak into it.

Norman Vincent Peale

CHAPTER 1

GETTING THE MOST OUT OF LIFE

NOT everybody views life alike. Some seem filled with the exciting elixir of existence. Others seem to drag like a rag mop. One fellow said, "When we were first married, my wife would wake me up with 'lo, the dawn'; now it is 'mow the lawn'!" A college student defined life as "the penalty you pay for the crime of being born." Not too exciting, huh?

And life is boring to some. They dread each day, and never look forward to a new one! Life to them is a meaningless cycle. They never go to bed with satisfaction, and they wake each morning without expectation.

And quality of life is not a "collection of things," but rather an attitude and a philosophy. It is the rules you live by. And success is a "journey" and not a "destination"!

I See Too Much Emptiness!

I scan the newspapers everyday as a "good-finder." I'm looking for stories and illustrations to pack my speeches on positive thinking and success. But I've got to confess, it takes some doing to get off page one. As Paul Harvey once said, "If it's not black, bleak or bloody, it doesn't get on page one." But by the time you've read the newspaper, watched the evening news, taken a look in your own neighborhood you see a lot of emptiness. People are asking, "Is this all there is?" There is loneliness and depression all over the place. Folks are not "living"; they are merely "existing."

Too Many Unnecessary Funerals!

I've done a lot of funerals in my thirty-six years of preaching. They were for folks ninety-six years old, down to stillborn. Several were teenagers. Twenty-eight percent were under fifty, and three were my own age. And I wonder how many of them died of their own choice? Oh, I don't mean suicide (though I've had a few of these). I mean where there was no reason for them to die. They died of neglect, self-abuse; of rules they broke. And they robbed themselves and their families of years of happiness and accomplishment.

In an article from Tulsa World (9-17-84) Dr. Richard Slagle listed five factors in heart attacks that struck men under 40. They were:

- High cholesterol

- Smoking

- Hypertension

- "30 to 45 year olds make up a significant portion of my practice"

- "Younger heart attacks tend to be smokers, diets high in fat, family history of heart disease"

Six things were listed in the article to "Reduce the risk of heart attack."

- Stop Smoking
- Eat Healthy Foods
- Exercise
- Keep Weight Down
- Reduce Stress
- Get Periodic Checkups

Would you please notice that all six of these are within our own power? Maybe you can't control some accidents or acts of God (such as tornado, flood, etc.). But it is a shame to see such a waste of America's greatest natural resource (the lives of its people), through things that could be controlled if we would just do it.

"Life: The Great, Unexplored Phenomenon"

Exploration is an exciting thing. We all love accounts of exploration of jungles, new lands, polar regions, space and sea. But I'm convinced the most exciting thing that has yet to be explored to its depths (or heights) is "Life" itself! Life is more beautiful than we know. Life has more blessings than we have enjoyed. Life has more opportunities and possibilities than we have ever imagined. And life is more within our own power than any of us have ever expected. Oh, to really be "alive"...alert...in tune...radiant...enthused...excited...expecting and achieving. Jesus said "I have come that you might have *life* and might *have it to the full*" (John 10:10)!

A New Campaign!

Too many people are missing out! So what do we propose to do about it? I, for one, am going to live it! I'm going to preach it. I'm going to teach it in my "Peak of the Week" class. I'm going to speak it in every seminar I give to businesses, church and civic groups all over America, and around the world.

In succeeding chapters of this book, we are going to tell you how to get the most out of your God-given body; how to develop relationships that are rewarding and meaningful. We'll discuss fitness, morality, mental and spiritual toughness that will enhance the beauty of life. We're going on a campaign to see that you, the reader, understand you've been put here on earth to grab all the gusto you can get. I believe you've been made in the image of God, and that God (your Father) wants you to know He owns it all; He wants you to have it all, and that His way insures that you enjoy it the most.

Climb aboard for an exciting journey to help you GET THE MOST OUT OF LIFE!

CHAPTER 2

THE ROAD TO ANYWHERE!

I was sitting on the edge of the hospital examining table when I saw it. It was a beautiful picture of a country road. It wound its way over the hills between lovely trees. It was picturesque. The sky was lovely; the scenery beautiful. It was the kind of picture that made you wish you were on that road, going wherever it was headed. And then I spotted the caption, "The Road to Anywhere, Starts Where You Are Right Now"! "Wow," I said. That's exactly what I needed at the moment. And I knew it would be one of my next lessons for the "Peak of the Week" class.

You see, I am a runner. But I'd been off my program a bit; picking up a few pounds, and I knew I needed a stress test. I knew that Hillcrest Hospital had a new H.E.L.P. program (Health Exercise Lifestyle Program). For only $75.00, they would give me a treadmill test, plus a bunch of other fitness evaluations. I lasted 12 minutes on the treadmill, and was puffing for dear life. On the hand gripping test, I got only a few marks out of "terrible." The nurse said, "Sit on that table, and we'll be back with your evaluations."

I needed that caption: "The road to anywhere, starts where you are right now." I knew I had been in peak condition for a 52-year-old. And it really is tough to try to whip back into shape after you let things go for a while. The picture, and that caption, reminded me of where I wanted to be. And it gave me assurance that I could get there, simply by starting right where I was. I could not make it in a single bound. But I could decide and begin, and if I held on course I could go anywhere I wanted to go! This of course is true of us all. You *can* do what you want to do; go where you want to go, and have what you want to have. It was the boost to get me going back to the fitness level I knew I wanted...and now I would have!

Glenn and his two brothers, Floyd and Raymond, and their sister, Letha, hurried the two miles to school that cold, windy morning in Rolla, Kansas, population 180. The year was 1916. Glenn was seven years old. The teacher hadn't arrived yet, so Floyd went over to the fireplace to start a fire. He poured what he thought was kerosene on the wood and struck a match. It wasn't kerosene. It was gasoline. There was a horrible explosion and Floyd screamed, "I'm on fire!" Glenn realized he was on fire too. They screamed for the other two to throw sand on them as they ran outside. But the ground was frozen. "We've got to get home," Floyd screamed. The other kids stared in horror. Floyd was virtually naked. The top of his jacket and smoking shoes were all that were left on his blackened body. Remembering the words of their father, "Never quit," they ran on in a frenzied effort to get where they could be helped.

Somehow they made it to the farmhouse. Glenn fainted within sight of the house. Floyd died shortly after. Glenn was burned terribly, and the doctor worked feverishly to save his life. The doctor said Glenn would never walk again. And if infection set in, he would have to amputate. But his condition grew worse. Infection *did* set in. Somehow they managed not to amputate, but the doctor reiterated that Glenn would never walk again. He overheard those terrible words and screamed, "I will. I will. I will walk again." His grieving mother said evenly, "Yes, Glenn, you'll walk again."

Then came months of daily treatments with ointment and salve. Glenn's father could run like the wind. He had said that Glenn was a natural. He taught him how to pump his arms and lengthen his stride so he could run longer and faster. He taught him how to pace himself for endurance. But now this seven-year-old boy was burned so badly, they said he'd never walk again.

It was six months after the accident that he tried his first step. But he fell in a heap. Another year, and he could walk a few steps. Later he could manage a limping jog.

His family moved to Elkhart, Kansas (population 1160). Within a year, Glenn could manage the two-mile walk to school. But he couldn't run without pain. By the time he was twelve, Glenn could run again. He entered the mile run in school. He was smaller than the other boys and didn't have the fancy running clothes they had. But he had something more! He used everything his father had taught him and won that one mile race.

Glenn Cunningham went on to become a great olympic champion. He was the outstanding miler of his day. He won twenty-one of thirty-one races in Madison Square Garden and set world records in the mile and 800 meters. At the end of his track career he established the Cunningham Youth Ranch where he and his wife helped thousands of troubled youth over a thirty year period. The road to anywhere starts where you are right now!

Wilma Rudolph knew about that road. She was twentieth out of twenty-two children, born to a struggling handyman. At the age of four she was stricken with scarlet fever and double pneumonia. It left her left leg paralyzed. They fitted her with a leg brace, but the prognosis was "she'll never walk again."

"I kept cheating," Wilma said. "I'd sneak off, take the brace off and test the leg." She was walking normally by the age of ten. She played basketball by age thirteen. At age sixteen Wilma Rudolph ran with the olympic relay team in Melbourn, Australia. The rest is public knowledge. In the 1960 Olympics she was the first woman ever to win three gold medals. She has won such awards as "Outstanding

Athlete of the Year," "Female Athlete of the Year," and was inducted into the Hall of Fame of Women's Sports Foundation. They did a two-hour prime time showing of her autobiography, "Wilma"!

The road to anywhere starts where you are right now!

The Bible is full of such stories. We've said before "Your past explains you; but it doesn't lock you in."

There is the story of Joseph, whom Chuck Swindoll calls, "From Pit to Pinnacle." It is the story of a boy who couldn't be kept down. He was favored by his father, hated by his brothers; sold as a slave into Egypt. And there, through no fault of his own, he was thrown into jail for an "attempted rape" which he did not "attempt." But he refused to give in to bitterness, self-pity and the "why me?" philosophy. His persistence in goodness and his unwavering faith in God led him to be promoted to second in command in Egypt, and the rescue of his entire family from poverty. This set up the entire scenario for the coming of the Lord Jesus Christ. Joseph started that journey upward from the depths of prison. Truly, the road to anywhere starts where you are right now!

Others come to mind. The story of David might be called "From Kid to King"; Saul's, "Opposer to Apostle." The Corinthian story, "Immoral to Immortal" (1 Cor. 6:9-11). And the story of John Mark, "From Deserter to Disciple." You can get knocked down, but you don't have to stay down!

Contemporary Examples

Our local newspaper, the Tulsa World, contained the story of Nadine Crow. She lost her right arm, and was therefore unable to continue her secretarial job. She and her daughters, Irene and Dee formed *"We Do It, Inc."* It was a business of helping people do things they needed done, but didn't want to do themselves. They admit to a few strange requests, including a few who wanted female companionship. And they've done a few strange things, like burying a dog, moving a piano, cleaning gutters, doing housework, moving households, conducting estate sales, hauling and raking. You name it, they've done it! They have referral services for plumbers, electricians, nurses aids, and a host of other needed services.

Nadine's tragedy dropped her to a pit she didn't want to be in. But she also knew "the road to anywhere starts where you are right now." And she is an inspiring example to the rest of us.

At the Garnett church, we've got lots of people who have learned this valuable lesson. *Sam Burton* is a multiple war veteran and hero. He's been in more battles and has more wounds than John Wayne. They did an amputation a few years back. Then they told him they'd have to amputate the other leg. Some time later he was back to amputate the first leg a little higher. But you couldn't keep Sam down. He walks on his prosthesis and a walker. He was down for the count. Knocked down, but not knocked out! He began right where he was. And today he is regular in attendance and is one of the happiest people in our church.

Bill Buchanan had an accident on the lake, which broke his neck. He had been a robust, active man. Doctors didn't think he'd live. But he has grabbed life with a grip that won't let go. He had to retrain in a field his paralyzed body could handle—accounting! He is my tax man; he drives his "Ironside" style van. He is productive and happy. He's my friend! He learned, "the road to anywhere starts where you are right now."

Harold Hillenburg, Sr. was a poor, oil field worker. Not much education. Not a brilliant future! But he believed in America. He believed in free enterprise. He bought an old used pipe threader, and began buying used pipe and selling to the oil fields. He bought up oil leases when everyone was selling. They didn't believe they were worth anything! Harold has stayed on that "road to anywhere" and is a literal "rags to riches" story. And all the time he has maintained his faith in his country, his God, his church and his family.

He is a living example to young businessmen today wondering what they can accomplish and where they can go. The road to anywhere starts where you are right now.

So, where *are* you? Where do you *want* to be? It doesn't matter where you've been or how many knocks life has given you. The road is there. The choice is yours. It leads where you want it to lead!

CHAPTER 3

TEACHING PELICANS HOW TO FISH!

MONTEREY, California has one of the best harbors on the West Coast. And they once had a thriving fishing industry there. Fishermen went out to sea, and hauled in tons of sardines. They had a big cannery right there in Monterey. There was also a huge colony of pelicans in Monterey—those funny looking birds with the big pouch under their bills. Pelicans ordinarily feed themselves by swooping down low over the water, and scooping up fish in their bills. But these pelicans were different. They didn't have to fly and hunt. They could eat their fill of fish heads and cleanings dropped over the sides of the fishing boats.

They had it made. Their food was literally brought to their doorstep. There was an abundance. They were all well fed, fat and happy. That is, until a sudden event changed the course of their lives.

World War II began for the United States with the bombing of Pearl Harbor. Shortly thereafter, Japanese submarines were spotted off the coast of California. There was fear of an invasion. The fishing industry was brought to a standstill. No boat wanted to risk being sunk. And now the pelicans had a problem.

You see, by now they had raised a whole generation of pelicans who didn't know how to fish. No one had taught them. They didn't have to. Why should they fly and swoop when there was plenty of food lying on the surface of the water, right in the harbor? The birds began to starve to death. People tried to feed them, but it wasn't enough. Soon scores of bodies of these great birds were lying all over the place. Many floated in the harbor itself. You can imagine the sight and smell! Now the city of Monterey had a problem. What to do with all these pelicans who didn't know how to fish? Just how do human beings go about teaching pelicans how to fish?

Finally some bright soul suggested these pelicans might learn to fish if they saw other pelicans fishing. After all, it was the natural thing for pelicans to do. St. Petersburg, Florida also had a large colony of pelicans. They captured and sent one hundred and fifty of the birds to Monterey. The Florida pelicans were turned loose and promptly started doing what pelicans do best—fishing! In no time at all, the California pelicans caught on, and were back in the act. There was plenty for all, the problem was solved, and everyone was happy. I see at least three powerful lessons in the story for us.

We Can Have Too Much Done For Us

We really don't need as much as we think we do. Our basic needs are very simple. We only need a small quantity of food. Most of us eat far too much anyway. And our requirements for shelter are simple. Most of us hardly need the luxurious homes in which we live. Now there is nothing wrong with luxury, unless you confuse it with "necessity." We need adequate clothing; hardly the fashion and surplus most of us enjoy. And we need nurturing and water. Everything beyond this is *luxury*! Things not necessary for survival, as two-thirds of the world can testify.

Indulgence can cripple us as it did those pelicans. Many of you have known, as I have, young people, crippled emotionally by being given too much. I knew a fine young man whose father told him, "You'll never have to work as hard as I did." The man had pulled himself up by his own bootstraps; had made a fortune, and vowed his kids would never have to work. The result was a boy so emotionally crippled he needed a job, but could not hold one. He simply had been given too much, and didn't know how to stand on his own.

All of us need a strong sense of personal responsibility. Yet how can we learn this when we turn all responsibility over to schools, the police and even the church! They are handy to blame if our siblings don't turn out the way they should. It is somehow "someone else's fault."

Remember the statement, "give a boy a fish, and he eats today; teach him to fish, and he will eat forever!"

I watched blue birds at our home teach their young how to fly. It seemed cruel. They urged the little ones out of the nest, onto the little perch, and nudged them off the edge. It was "fly or die." And, you know, not one of them died. It gave them the motivation to do what birds are supposed to do naturally. But take away their necessity for flying, and in a matter of time, birds won't fly. Someone has said, "blessing, without personal sacrifice, is crippling to us."

OPPORTUNITY IS ALWAYS THERE!

Monterey harbor abounded with fish. There was enough for every pelican in the area; enough for a national convention of pelicans. Opportunity wasn't the problem.

And our world, our nation, abounds with opportunity. There are those who feel there is no opportunity for them. They think there are no jobs and no chance. They whine, and blame everyone and everything they can think of. But the world is basically the same as it has always been. Things like inflation and depression, war and peace, corruption and ethics in government. In every generation there are paupers and millionaires. "One man's limp is another man's leap." It isn't the "times," as much as what you do about the times.

Opportunity is always there. Someone said "there has never been a depression that a million good salesmen couldn't cure."

LIfe is a "do-it-to-yourself" job. We have millions of unemployed while in every city, USA, the newspapers scream with "help wanted." I have located jobs for lots of so-called "job seekers," only to have them tell me, "that's not the kind of job I want," or worse yet, "I can make more on welfare than working there." Such a person is a parasite on society, and will never be happy or a success!

Opportunity is always there. Opportunity for making a living. Opportunity for happiness. Happiness is always in abundance. The Bible makes it clear that early Christians were radiantly happy. Yet this was in the midst of Roman captivity, slavery and immorality of gigantic proportion. Happiness is not a set of circumstances; it is a decision and attitude of the heart. It is this attitude that finds opportunity; takes life by the horns, and makes it work.

Associate With Winners!

All the plans failed to feed the pelicans or teach them to fish. They tried hand feeding. Nothing worked. Finally the plan to "import some winners" (those Florida pelicans) worked. It is a tremendous idea to surround the needy with "winners." Let them witness success. Let them know that what "one pelican can do, another can too."

Humans tend to become like the people with whom they associate. Losers associate with other losers, and become losers. But the opposite is also true. I heard this advice given to young men who wanted to become successful and prosperous; "take a rich man to lunch, and you pay for it."

The rules for success are "identifiable" and "learnable." If you "pick the brains" of successful men and women, you'll pick up their secrets. And you'll be surprised to learn that the things they did to become successful are within your own ability to employ.

The Bible says, "Bad company corrupts good character" (1 Cor. 15:33). Our jails and prisons are full today of people whose start to ruin was in "hanging aroung with the wrong crowd." But the opposite is also true. If you associate with the good, the moral, the ethical, men and women of integrity, ambition and a positive attitude, you'll become like them. You'll perform like them. And you'll enjoy the benefits they enjoy. It is so important to associate with "winners!"

Well, the Monterey pelicans are a good story. Their problem was solved, and the situation is going great. But it doesn't compare with the good that will be done if you learn these lessons and apply them to your lives.

1. Don't ask others to do for you, when you can do for yourself.
2. Wake up and see opportunity all around you.
3. Associate with winners.

And you'll start receiving more benefits than you ever thought possible.

CHAPTER 4

COWBOYS DON'T WALK HOME!

"WE are hard pressed on every side; but not crushed. Perplexed, but not in despair. Persecuted but not abandoned. Struck down but not destroyed" (2 Cor. 4:8, 9).

The apostle Paul was an amazing man. Besides being one of the great New Testament leaders, he was hit by more problems than most see in a lifetime. Scripture reveals that he had a horrible disease that probably affected his appearance and eyesight. He had been thrown in prison, received the Roman thirty-nine lashes on five different occasions. He had been beaten with rods, stoned and left for dead, shipwrecked, abandoned, and robbed. On top of all that he had the daily care of the churches. He was not invincible. He simply knew that cowboys don't walk home. They get thrown off, stomped on, bruised, broken and dirty. But they get up, climb back on, and ride home! Paul didn't know how to quit. That's what made him a winner. That's what makes winners today!

Orville Peterson, Olympic Cowboy

We read with interest Randy Galloway's column on the young man from Baptist Campbell College in North Carolina. Orville Peterson was a representative for the United States in the decathlon. After the first day of competition in this ten-event competition, Orville had been in a solid eighth place. But in day two, in the 110 meter high hurdles, Orville pulled muscles and ligaments in his left thigh. It seemed obvious to all, that this splendid athlete would have to drop out of the competition. He refused even to visit the trainer for fear he'd make him drop out. So he went on competing in discus, somehow managed to pole-vault 12'5", and even throw the javelin 206'9". But under those circumstances, even though his efforts were valiant, it dropped him to 14th place. Only the 1,500 meter run was left. And just how was this young man with torn muscles and ligaments going to make it, four laps around the track?

But he ran! His thigh was wrapped heavily! He promised himself he'd finish this run no matter how long it took.

There were 21,000 spectators in the stands for this event. The race was run and over. Only about 300 people remained in the stands. But one lone runner staggered on. He would not quit. He limped toward the finish. The small crowd in the stands began to cheer him on. Fellow contestants lined the track and began to cheer him on. From over the loud speaker in the coliseum came the theme from "Chariots of Fire."

Suddenly this event was bigger than any other in the Olympics. It seemed to have more significance than world records and gold medals; even which country might come out the overall winner. As Peterson ran those last few yards, the announcer over the P.A. system read this Greek saying:

"Never ask for victory; ask only for courage. For if you endure the struggle, you bring honor to yourself. But most important, you bring honor to us all."

Somehow Orville Peterson knew "cowboys don't walk home!"

Other Cowboys!

While we're thinking about the Olympics, there were two other cowboys (or maybe I should say cowgirls) of great significance in the first ever women's marathon. Now you understand there have been many races both mixed and women's marathons, but this was the first time the women's marathon was included in the Olympics. A cowgirl came in first, and a cowgirl came in last.

Joan Benoit won the gold. Joan doesn't know the meaning of "quit." Just a few days before the Olympic trials in the United States she had orthoscopic surgery on her knee. She won the trials and then won a "hands down," "nobody close" victory in the Olympics itself. She knew that "cowboys don't walk home."

I doubt that many will remember the name of the Swiss contestant. But few will ever forget that pathetic figure, completely exhausted, who came in last. She staggered all over the track. She fought off those who rushed out to help her, for to touch her would have disqualified her. She ran valiantly beyond her own ability till she collapsed across the finish line. Hers was a victory as sure as the gold belonged to Joanie. Cowboys don't walk home!

Alan Shepherd was our first sub-orbital astronaut. Possibly more people watched that initial flight, over 20 years ago, than watch the current space flights on television. It was news then. And many believed it could not be done. But he went up, 150 miles and made successful re-entry into the earth's atmosphere, and his capsule parachuted to a safe landing in the ocean. But you see, Alan Shepherd had a higher goal. He wanted to be one of the men to walk on the moon. But tragedy struck. He developed health problems, and he was assigned to a desk job. He became a great success in the business world, but the dream still lived in the man. He underwent surgery. It was a long road back, but he regained his health, got back in the space program, and finally made that successful trip to the moon. Not all those millions who heard his words, broadcast back from the moon's surface, would understand as he and his wife understood when he said, "It's been a long journey; but I'm here!" He was saying, "Cowboys don't walk home!"

Persistence: The Key To Character And Success

Dr. Tex Goin, a Tulsa Cardiologist, authored a great little book entitled, *"Smile, or I'll Kick Your Bed!"* He remarks that you get all kinds of surprises in heart bypass surgery. Some who should make it by all right, don't! And some you wouldn't think had a chance, survive! It is this *tenacity*, this refusal to die...this will to live, that makes all the difference in the world! The power of our wills to influence success, happiness and even *"LIFE"* is simply amazing.

And it's more than skill, ability, training or the "breaks." It works in business, marriage, churches and individual lives. Has fate kicked you in the teeth? Have you cried out in despair, "why me?" You can wallow in self-pity. You can scream that it isn't fair. But who said life had to be "fair!" You say you're not the "wrong-er;" you're the wrong-ee;" and the dirty rat that done it to you is scot free! But what will wallowing get you?

Thomas Edison was a cowboy. As he searched for a filament that would stay lit, someone asked him how many experiments he'd tried. "Oh, about 3,000," was his reply. "How can you keep going when you've had 3,000 failures? To which the great Edison angrily replied, "Failures? I've had no failures. I've learned 3,000 ways it can't be done. I'm getting closer all the time." And after approximately 10,000 such experiments, the lights are on all over the world. Cowboys don't quit. They get up, dust off, climb back on. And win the prize!

Aren't you glad Edison didn't quit after 9,000 experiments? Aren't you glad Wilbur and Orville didn't quit after the first flying machine wouldn't get off the ground? Aren't you glad the early American settlers didn't run from the Indians? Or give up the fight for freedom from foreign tyranny? I'm so glad my mother and dad didn't give up after having only three children.

You have to be taught quitting. It's not the natural thing to do. God protected us as babies or we'd never have learned to walk, talk, dress ourselves or eat with knives and forks. We failed so many times, but we kept going. Later in life, folks were taught to cry and quit after a few failures. Maybe Jesus had some of that in mind when He said, "Except you become as little children, you shall not enter into the Kingdom of Heaven."

Winston Churchill is remembered for many things. Surely one of the greatest statesmen England ever had. He was a good friend of our own President Franklin Delano Roosevelt, and great ally of the United States. But perhaps the greatest speech he ever made, surely one he is most remembered for, is the one delivered for the boys school, his old alma mater. The boys were all instructed to take notes on this great man's speech, for he was reputed to be one of the greatest orators in the world.

The 5'2", 250 pound "Winnie" walked before the audience of admiring boys. "Nevah," he said. "Nevah!" "Nevah Quit!"

"Cowboys don't walk home!"

CHAPTER 5

THREE DIMENSIONAL LOVE!

LOVE is the greatest thing in the world! It's what makes the world go around! If your life is full of love, you are rich indeed! If you miss it, no matter what else you possess, you are extremely poor! Someone wrote, "better never to have lived, than never to have loved." And love is three-dimensional!

You've Got To Love Yourself!

One of the experts in the law once asked Jesus, "What is the greatest commandment in the Law?" (Mt. 22:36-40). His reply was startling. It contained the following information:
1. Love God with all your heart.
2. Love your neighbor as you love yourself.
3. All the law hangs on these two commandments.

It would be pretty easy for all "Bible-reading" folks to agree we should love God. And not much extra effort is necessary to understand we should love others. But this next part *"as yourself"* sneaks up on us.

We can only give away *what we possess*! You can only love others if you love yourself. And we don't mean conceit. Someone defined conceit as "that disease that makes everyone sick except the person who has it!" People shy away from affirming that they love themselves. And as a matter of fact, just a shallow study will reveal that there is precious little "self love" going around.

People are "down on themselves." Low self image is common, especially in those who cover it with a "brash, intimidation." Some of the loudest, harshest, braggarts suffer from low self esteem. And in a study by a Northeastern University of over 600 psychology majors, they revealed that most are gripped by a common fear that they "don't have what it takes."

We conceal this by wearing all kinds of masks. We all wear them, you know. We all put on the "good front." The more I know you, the more I love you, the more masks I take off. But I never take off the last one. For I am afraid that if I let you see me as I really am...and you don't like me...I am ruined! Why are we so afraid for people to know us completely? Isn't it this deep-seated fear that we may not be acceptable?

Now back to the text. If we are to love our neighbors "as ourselves," doesn't it naturally follow, that we are to love ourselves? Jesus sees worth in us all! Isn't that good news? Doesn't that "peak you week?" I sometimes instruct my class to give themselves a "self hug" and repeat after me,
"I LOVE YOU, YOU SWEET OLD THING!"
It always causes lots of laughter, but they enjoy it. We would all enjoy it, for we want so badly to be able to love ourselves.

You see, you *really are* "Lovable!" You *were* born with that ribbon wrapped around you, reading, "I am lovable and capable!" And self-love is essential to being able to love anyone or anything else!

Following this Biblical line of reasoning, husbands are also instructed to "Love your wives as you *love yourself*" (Eph. 5:28). There's the key to a lot of marital troubles. If you really love yourself, it is easy to love your mate; difficulty in loving your mate, may be rooted in a lack of "self-love!"

And then I read that "God loves me" (John 3:16). He can't be wrong about me, can He? If God sees worth in me, must

I argue with this, or can I allow myself to believe that I am worth something? That I am really a very valuable person? Oh, what this does for self-esteem! And what self-esteem does for our attitudes and relationships with others.

Develop A Love For God!

It is only when we come to grips with love for ourselves, that we can develop a love for God! And what is love for God based upon? It is based upon the fact that we have been created in God's image (Gen. 1:26). And seeing it was "not good for man to live alone" (Gen. 2:18) He created woman; and marriage. And then the kids come. And with this constant outpouring of the love and providence of God, we cannot keep from shouting, "Wow, isn't God wonderful?"! He geared the whole universe to our needs and desires. The seasons, the laws of nature, the natural resources are entirely for our enjoyment.

David exclaims, "I am fearfully and wonderfully made" (Psa. 139:14)! When you just ponder our marvelous senses of touch, sight, hearing, smelling and tasting; it just boggles our imagination a God who could think all this up!

And then comes "free choice." Probably God's greatest gift to us is this ability to choose for ourselves. No one can make you do wrong, if you want to do right; and no one can make you do right, if you choose to do wrong. The possibilities of that are staggering. But we "blew that one." And Jesus came to save us from our self-caused ruin! Can you love a God like that?

Love For Others!

The first two "loves" spill over into love and service for others. The basis is "self-love!" There will be no love for God until you have some measure of love for self. Self-love naturally develops your love for God for He is responsible for all you have and are! The two together, give you a feeling for, a "reaching out" to others. "If God so loved us, we ought to love one another" (I John 4:11). Love for others is a natural reaction of love of self, and love for God. It is the "fruit" of the "loving tree!"

The Bible says, "love you neighbor" as yourself; "Love your wife" as your own body. So love begins to branch out. It begins to find its joy in seeking the well-being of others.

You are urged to give yourself unreservedly, unconditionally to those worthy of your love. Give tenderness, thoughtfulness and compassion to others. For they are objects of God's love the same as you.

"Do everything in love" (I Cor. 16:14)! Oh, if we only treated one another in this way.

I was attending a banquet in Indianapolis. A man came up to the head table where I was seated and shared this lovely story with me. It blessed my life. I hope it will bless yours. He said, he and his son were at a "father/son" retreat, with several other Christians. Someone spoke on that moving scripture where Jesus washed his disciples' feet. It was suggested that each father and son wash each other's feet as an act of love and humility; and to capture some of the marvelous attitude of our Savior. The boy knelt at his father's feet, took off his shoes, and slowly, tenderly began washing and rubbing his father's feet. With tears in his eyes he said, "Dad, I'm not as good a boy as you think I am!" With equal emotion, and voice choked with love, the father replied, "Son, I'm not as good a man as you think I am." I wept with the joy and closeness I knew this father and his son had experienced. I instinctively knew the closer relationship they would have as a result of that outpouring of love between them.

Don't you see the absolute necessity of love? Don't you see that to develop love in our lives, it must follow this three step process...love of self, love of God, and then love for others!

May God give you the power to put this love to work in your life. Don't let pride, bashfulness or anything stand in your way. Claim love today. And claim it "three dimensional!"

CHAPTER 6

A YEAR OF OCTOBERS!

DON'T you just love October? It is Dot's favorite month. I must confess it is mine too. Oh, we love Spring too. God really turns it on in October. You ought to take advantage of October, especially if yours is anything like those in Tulsa, Oklahoma.

There's nothing like a weiner roast on Spunky Creek. I've had my entire "Peak of the Week" class out at our house, around a big open fire, making hot dogs, sipping lemonade,and really enjoying a lovely October night. The air is crisp, and nature paints a masterpeice of the landscape in October.

And leaves! Oh, yes, the leaves. I share Leo Buscaglia's love of leaves. There ought to be a law against raking leaves. And for goodness sakes, never burn them! Leaves are to dance in, walk and run through, throw in the air, throw at each other, roll in; but never to rake or burn!

You've got special energy in October. You feel like taking walks, looking at the grey sky. And when God gives an "Indian Summer," it just makes it that much more beautiful.

October brings football games, Thanksgiving, Halloween, homecoming, and a host of other things. Thank God for October. Why can't it last?

But some things are seasonal. They come and go. And I'm sure I wouldn't want it any other way. We spent seven years in Australia, and our family enjoyed Christmas, which came right in the middle of the summer. Oh, they still sang all the Christmas carols, "Jingle Bells," "I'm Dreaming of a White Christmas," but the weather was 100+ outside. But the seasons come and go there the same as in America. It's the way it should be! I really don't want to swim in the lake in February, or cuddle by the fireplace in July. Seasons come and go. And life is like that! The Spring of Youth soon gives way to the Summer of Maturity. Fall comes and Winter is not far away, and before you know it, life has gone! Opportunity and health pass like the seasons.

But why not make October last? It's a nice month. Let's not give it up without a fight. In the Garnett Church of Christ where I minister we sing "There is Sunshine in My Soul Today" while it is raining outside. And we explain that sunshine lives in the Christian no matter what the weather is like outside. Maybe in the same way we can perpetuate October. Let's pass around a petition to make October last all year long. Want to sign? October forever!!!

Well, October will give way to November no matter what we do. But the really good things of life we want, we can have anytime. All the time! Let's look at a few.

How about walks? They are season-less. Walks in October are nice, but you can have them in February or July. You just dress differently. I do it with jogging. On a 90-degree, hot summer morning I ran in shorts and a shirt. In January at 15° I went out for a run. I counted seventeen pieces of clothing as I undressed. But I confess I enjoyed both runs. The same is true with good food, good company, sports and everything! If you just make a few adjustments for different conditons, you can do just about anything you want to do, in any kind of season or weather.

And then there's laughter. You can always have laughter. You get it when you play with babies (your own or someone else's). You can read good books, watch good movies, and enjoy the company of friends. There is fun, entertainment and games available any time you want them.

Friendship is always available. There are no seasons on reunions. You can plan to be together any time you want. You can "reach out and touch someone" by telephone. And friends are so important. Stay in touch with good friends.

Romance is ageless. It is seasonless. It is always in demand. The young have no corner on romance. You will need it as long as you live. And thank God, it is always around, always in demand, never in short supply. Affection is so needed in our lives. The Bible urges us to be "Kindly affectioned one toward the other" (Rom. 12:10). We need hugs, kisses, positive strokes, encouraging words, and gifts of thoughtfulness and love. We must bid October farewell till next year. But these things can go on (they *must* go on) all the time.

Love is an ageless, seasonless quality. It is the greatest thing in the world. It is a pity we show the least love to the ones we love the most. Someone said that to make life worth living, "you must love someone worth loving; and hold on to something big enough to hold you." Someone else said, "Better never to have lived than never to have loved." Love makes the world go around.

And then there's God! God is God of October; but He is also the God of July and April. The Bible urges "be instant in season, out of season" (2 Tim. 4:2-4). Wouldn't it be sad, yea tragic, if we had to say goodbye to God till next season? But God is always there; He always loves, always cares, always blesses, and always receives those who come by faith to Him.

His Church is His Family! And the Church is always there to those who need "Family." Many are downtrodden, broken, bruised and bleeding. They need to know someone is there to care. It is a comfort to know the church is always there. Salvation is there. A personal relationship with God and His people is always there.

The Bible says "Enoch walked with God; and he was no more, because God took him away" (Gen. 5:24). A little boy was trying to put this story into his own words. "God and Enoch," he said, "were good friends. They often took long walks together. They would just talk and talk. Sometimes they would lose all track of time. One day they were out walking. They walked and walked and talked and talked. All of a sudden Enoch looked up and said, 'God, it's getting late. I'd better head for home.' But God said, 'Enoch, we're closer to My house than to yours. Why don't you come on and go home with Me?' So Enoch went home with God." Not a bad story. And pretty accurate too.

What we're saying, dear reader, is that the really great things of life can be had all the time. Like a year of Octobers. Make sure you get your share!

CHAPTER 7

DON'T KNOCK RE-RUNS!

ANN Landers is a favorite of mine. I read her column every morning and have done so for years. She was recently criticized for "re-cycling" her columns; that is, using some of the same letters again. Ministers and other speakers do it all the time. And they do it intentionally. I heard Cavett Robert say that in order for a speech to be really professional you must give it five hundred times. I know if a farmer has a good plow, he will use it more than one time! From church bulletins, I see the terms "selected," "adapted," and "borrowed" appear time after time. If a thing is worth hearing, it is worth hearing again.

How many times have you seen "Gone With the Wind"? One lady said, "I cried the last two times I saw it, and I'm gonna cry again the next time." I heard our daughter, Tammy, say "Chariots of Fire" was better the second time. And I must confess, I watch all those old re-runs of "M-A-S-H" over and over again.

The Garnett Church of Christ, where I am pulpit minister, has a song book containing over seven hundred songs. But we consistently use about twenty of these. We can sing them from memory. But they describe the character and ministry of this church. And we can really belt them out! We like it better than new ones every time.

But there's a negative feeling about "repetition." Someone says, "I read a book on positive thinking *ONCE*!" Or, I've heard that speaker, or that speech before. That's like the lady who heard that sleeping on feathers would promote restful sleep...so she tried *"one"*! Repetition in reading, hearing, viewing is like eating. You must eat more than one time. It's like bathing, you need to do it over and over!

In the Bible, the terms "remember," "remind" and "remembrance" appear almost three hundred times. The words carry with them the meaning of "returning to mind," "bringing back to conscious memory what had been there before." You see, we tend to forget. And yet we act on what we know; what is currently in our memory. Thus the need to recall, "remember again."

The Bible uses this form of teaching over and over again.
"Remember what the Lord did" (Deut. 24:9).
"I thank God every time I remember you" (Phil. 1:3).
"Do this in remembrance of me" (1 Cor. 11:24, 25).
"I say it (to you) again" (Gal. 1:8, 9).
"I write the same things to you again" (Phil. 3:1).
"This is my second letter; both of them are reminders,
to stimulate you to wholesome thinking" (2 Pet. 3:1).
Wow! That last verse really grabs you, doesn't it!? Repetition! Re-runs! Reminding you over and over again. This is the way to stimulate you to "wholesome thinking." I know you will agree we could use lots more "wholesome thinking." And the key, is reminding you again and again! Re-runs!

When you think of it, re-runs are the best way of learning anything. Anyone who does anything well, has used repetition! One lady listened with rapt attention to a concert pianist! She later said to him, "I'd give half my life to be able to play as you do." To which he replied, "That's exactly what I did give!" Most of us who see the final product, do not realize the hours and years that were given to be able to perform flawlessly! A professional athlete has literally given years of doing the same thing, over and over again, to acquire his skill. Thousands of trial runs preceded Carl Lewis' single hundred meter dash for the gold medal at the 1984 Olympics in Los Angeles. Mary Lou Retton did the same routine again and again to develop the form that made her a gold medal winner in gymnastics. But it is also true with machinists, doctors, cooks and painters. In fact anyone who does anything well knows the path of routine. Re-runs!

A baby learns to walk through re-runs. There is that shaky "first step." It is exciting to parents, but would hardly win a medal in competition. There is a lot of wobbling and falling. There is a lot of getting up and trying again. Only after months of such trial and error can children finally master the art of walking.

And then, just think of that terrible ordeal of learning to "feed yourself!" Bill Cosby did a routine on the philosophy behind the way babies eat. Bill figured it was a whole different method of nutrition. Mashed potatoes were patted on top of the head. English peas were poked into the ears. Milk runs down the chin and into the stomach through the belly button.

Well, you get the picture! But the truth is, babies only learn to eat properly by "try and try again." Re-runs!

It is said Thomas Edison tried approximately 10,000 experiments in an effort to develop a filament that would hold a light. After about 3,000 of these, an interested person asked him, "How can you continue to try, after so many failures?" To which Edison hotly replied, "I've never failed in my life. I've already found 3,000 ways it can't be done. I'm getting closer every day!" Re-runs!

By this same method we've come from the model-T to the Rolls Royce. From the Wright brothers' first aircraft to space rockets that put men on the moon. We've come from the loin cloth to Brooks Brothers suits, from caves to cathedrals.

The Power Of Repetition

Many people worry because they can't remember scripture! Now it is nice to memorize Bible verses. But Jesus said, "Now you are *clean* by the word I have spoken" (John 15:3). So read it again and again. Maybe you can't memorize it, but it will cleanse your heart and life.

This is called "spaced repetition" among professional speakers. They tell us that by listening to a cassette tape we pick up *information* up to sixteen times; but *inspiration* countless times. By the time you've heard a selected cassette recording seven times, you are already subconsciously thinking the way it has taught you. This has a powerful impact on your life. But be careful, for it has the same effect whether good or bad. This should make us very careful in the movies we choose to watch. The television shows we select. Even the books and magazines we buy. And especially in the company we keep. The Bible says, "Bad company corrupts good character" (1 Cor. 15:33).

But it naturally follows that if you carefully select the things you are going to do, read and view, you can control the direction and quality of your life. I therefore recommend regular church attendance, daily Bible reading, and regular reading of books and listening to tapes that will bring out your best, and urge you to success!

You say you've heard it all before? And tried it once? Well, if it was good, and something worth doing, do it again! Listen some more! Keep learning, for "as long as you're green, you'll grow, but when you're ripe, you'll rot!" Try another way! Set a newer and higher goal! Don't quit! Persistence and repetition are the keys to success!

DON'T KNOCK RE-RUNS!

CHAPTER 8

HOW TO BE "UP" WHEN YOU'RE "DOWN"!

THE "People Plus" rally in Lubbock, Texas, was over. I had had the good fortune of being on the program along with Dr. Norman Vincent Peale, Zig Ziglar and Cavett Robert. I took the same plane home that Dr. Peale and his lovely wife, Ruth, were on. We were talking about how everyone seemed to enjoy the rally. And about how we wish we could perpetuate that positive attitude on a daily basis. Dr. Peale said, "you mean how to be 'up' when you're 'down'!" We talked longer about this needed subject. I knew it would be my next speech in my "Peak of the Week" class back in Tulsa.

Did you ever want to quit? You see, it is easy to be up when things are going right. But, boy, can they go wrong! I can really get motivated and excited when folks are treating me good, complimenting my sermons and speeches, and writing notes of praise to me. But then I get passed by for a promotion, friends start taking me for granted, problems and obstacles show up, and I'm into a "pity party." "Somebody done me wrong," I sing, and my attitude is lower than a snake's belly.

I read about a preacher in the Bible who wanted to quit. Jeremiah (Jer. 9:1, 2; 20:7-9) wanted to quit. He had bad names for the people of his congregation. They were a worthless, useless, immoral bunch of wretches. He figured he'd go into the motel business. He even accused God of lying to him and deceiving him. He wanted to quit...but found he *couldn't*! There was a compulsion in him. He called it a "fire in my bones." That compulsion rallied him. A great man and a great ministry was saved because a man learned how to be "up" when he was "down!"

Life is full of "ups" and "downs!" There's the motion of the sea. The temperature in most places has its "highs" and "lows" (few climates are steady year round). Seasons change. Music would be monotonous without the "ups" and "downs" on the scale. Even the stock market would lose its customer appeal, if everything stayed the same. Whether high or low, it all stays a flat desert if it is all the same. Even your blood pressure rate has a diastolic and a systolic. If that figure ever gets to the same level, you'll pass out. So what about "ups" and "downs"; and what do we do about them?

Downs are "normal!" They come to everyone in all circumstances. The Bible says, "such things must come," referring to problems and obstacles. It also admonishes us, "no temptation has seized you, except what is common to man" (1 Cor. 10:13). You are not unique! We live in a negative world, filled with problems! Yet it is not the "downs," but our "reaction" to them, that makes all the difference in the world.

Downs are not the "whole story!" No one has all downs! Yet to hear some talk, that's all they have. One of my favorite points (I make it in just about all the speeches I give) is that we all have "two lists"; "reasons to be happy," and "reasons to be sad." Everyone in the world has these two lists. And when you are asked, "how are you?" you simply, subconsciously choose *which list* you'll tell them about. So you say "I feel great," or "I'm going to make it." But the truth is, both lists are there. Downs are not the whole story!

Downs are not permanent! I like the Bible verse that reads, "Let us not become weary in doing good, for at the proper time we will reap a harvest if we do not give up" (Gal. 6:9). Two verses earlier is that famous saying, "we reap what we sow." This promotes what I like to call the *"Three Laws of Sowing and Reaping!"* Mind you, I said, *"Laws"* (not theories or possibilities). They are (1) You reap *what* you sow, (2) You reap *more* than you sow, and (3) You reap *later* than you sow. Hang in there. Downs are not permanent. What you've sown, will soon come to the top!

Downs make the contrast! You couldn't see the white, except for the black; and vice-versa. Diamonds are best shown against black velvet. You can best appreciate the good times, if you hang in there during the bad times. A honeymoon every day, for the rest of your life, would be unreal, and finally unfulfilling. There are challenges to tackle, problems to solve, goals to accomplish. There's the vitality in living.

Downs are not the outcome! Many a team was behind at the half, and came back to win the game. By now we're all familiar with Doug Flutie's last minute "hail Mary," ball-in-the-air, gun-ending-the-game pass that won the game for Boston College. Or Chiminade University, Honolulu, where the ball went out of bounds and the clock stopped with "zero" seconds showing and Chiminade one point behind. But no buzzer had sounded to end the game. Chiminade got the ball out of bounds. The clock would start when the ball touched the hands of the inbounds receiver, who immediately hoisted the ball upwards. The buzzer sounded, ending the game; but the ball went through the hoop and Chiminade won the game. They were "down," but not "out!" It is not a crime to be "down"; only to "stay down!"

Well, finally, what do we do about downs? First of all, I suggest we *"accept them!"* As you might accept day and night; the time of day, the day of the week, the month of the year. Accept them as you accept the alarm clock that goes off at 6 a.m. It is simply that time, and there's nothing you can do about it. Get up, get going, nothing is fatal! You can handle it! There's nothing fatal about "downs," unless you surrender to them.

Secondly, *understand them!* "Downs" have never stopped anyone from success, whether in sports, career, marriage or church. You ask couples married for 50 years or longer, "were there any problems?" That will provoke a chuckle! Of course there were. But it didn't stop a great marriage from succeeding. Were there any business setbacks? Of course. But it is infinitely more important what you do *about* your problems. Problems won't stop any good thing from happening, if you understand them!

Thirdly, *"choose" to be UP!* The common question, "How do you feel?" is more accurately asked, "How do you *choose* to feel?" Life is what you choose it to be! Your world is what you choose it to be! Some gripe about conditions in the world, blame them for their failures. But isn't it peculiar? Many live in the same world, cope with the same problems, and come out on top. Choice, must have something to do with it. You can choose to be "up!" Dale Carnegie said, "To have a feeling, you must grab the feeling." Choose, therefore, happiness, health, success; and more importantly, choose Eternal Life! Affirm what you really want to be. So repeat these words at the top of your voice:

> I am made in God's Image!
> I can choose my attitude!
> I CHOOSE TO FEEL GREAT!

CHAPTER 9

NEVER ORDER VANILLA!

I walked into a Baskin-Robbins the other day, and stood dazzled by all those ice cream flavors. Did you ever hear such names, or see such combinations? Rocky Road, Apricot Brandy Yogurt, Peanut Butter, Bubblegum, Fudge Ripple, Banana Nut, Black Cherry Walnut, and dozens of others. It is a major event just making a choice! It boggles the mind and tantalizes the taste buds. Can you imagine anyone walking into such a place, amid all those flavors, and ordering "vanilla"? I mean, you can get vanilla *anywhere*. Every *grocery store* carries vanilla. This is a connoisseurs' ice cream parlor. Get on with the exciting, exotic flavors!

Life is like that. It is full of fantastic things to see, to learn and to do. There are things to enjoy, to play with; there are challenges and opportunities. There are goals to reach, and people to love. It is a wide, wonderful world out there. Yet many people step up to the counter of life and say, "gimme a half-gallon of 'bland';" "give me a double dip of mediocre;" "give me a cheap, boring sundae, covered with BLAH!"

Life was meant to be zestful, adventurous and exciting! I look in the Bible, and the heroes there took life by the horns, and really had a time. Joshua and Caleb were the two spies who said Canaan could be taken, whereas the other ten spies spoke of obstacles, and taking the safe, sane way out. God finally was about to give them the land when, forty years later, folks finally decided to follow Joshua and Caleb's advice. Even then, Caleb said, "I am 85 years old today. I am as strong as I ever was. Give me the land where the giants are. God and I can handle it." (Josh. 14:10-12). Ah, to have zest and energy like that. To believe, to challenge and act like that into old age, that would be great. No vanilla for Caleb!

David wasn't a "vanilla" man! He wrote, "This is the day the Lord has made; let us rejoice and be glad in it!" (Ps. 118:24).

And Jesus wasn't a mediocre man! His life did not "peak" and then level off. He was never "over the hill," and will never be a "has been!" Nor should you!

The New Testament speaks of happiness and joy and love! "Be joyful always (1 Thess. 5:16). "But the fruit of the Spirit is love, joy, peace, patience, kindness, goodness, faithfulness, gentleness and self-control" (Gal. 5:22). And get this classic, "Though outwardly we are wasting away, yet inwardly we are being renewed day by day" (2 Cor. 4:16).

But in spite of this many are "old at 33!" You see, age, depression and boredom are more of an attitude than circumstance." What does it mean to be "old at 33"? It means the twinkle is gone; you've lost the wonder. You've become "predictable." Spontaneity has vanished. The spirit of adventure has died in you: Romance is gone. There's nothing "new" in you. Therefore, the flavor has gone and you are left with "vanilla!"By the mid-thirties you have stopped acquiring skills and attitudes. You are "set in your ways," and it remains to push the corpse into the grave. Again, Cavett Robert says, "Lord, don't let me die, till I'm dead!"

We all need to restore enthusiasm to our soul. The very word, "enthusiasm" is an exciting word. It is taken from the Greek words "en" and "Theos" (the latter meaning God). Literally enthusiasm is "God in you," or "full of

God." The person "full of God" is going to be alive, vibrant and radiant. We could stand a huge dose of this in our world today!

We all need to break the mold of "predictability!" The "I Never Knew You Liked Piña Coladas" song (see chapter by that title), shows the need. Life can become boring; marriage can be "predictable." You can always pump new life into old marriages. This might be called "Giving your marriage mouth-to-mouth resuscitation."

You probably put your clothes on the same way, in the same order each morning. You drive to work by the same route. You approach problems in the same way. Even your sex life can become ritualistic, boring and predictable.

One guy said, "Well, you can't teach an old dog new tricks!" So isn't it great we're not dogs! And putting zest in your life is certainly not a trick! So we're off and running!

Begin tomorrow morning. Drive to work a new way. Maybe even 30 minutes earlier. Now that might really affect your attitude! Go to a new place for lunch. Try out a little "praise and compliments" on your work mates, boss or employees. Do something with your mate or family tonight. Don't always do the practical, the sensible. Sometimes it puts new zip into life by doing something on the spur of the moment; something that is exciting and fun, and really would bring happiness and joy into your own life or other people's lives.

But "breaking out" can also be dangerous. We are such extremists! I don't mean you ought to row to Hawaii in a four-foot dinghy. You don't have to dye your hair, buy a gold chain, and hang a shark's tooth around your neck. A lot of men in "mid-life crisis" get themselves a motorcycle. I don't mean for you to do something immoral, illegal, or contrary to God's will. Remember God is your friend! His way is the best way to live; and the only way to die! His way will give you all the zest you can handle. Just simply recognize that God (your Father) wants His kids happy...getting in on all the good stuff. Don't miss out on anything

He wants you to have!

Dr. James Dobson talks about the "straight life." We all live there, and at times it gets boring. Voices call us off the straight life; voices like "pleasure," "romance," "sex" and "ego." We run off after these and end up in awful ruin. But you see these "voices" *belong* in the "straight life." You don't break up a marriage, or give away your kids, or turn your back on God to have fun. With your face toward God, and both hands grabbing life by the horns is the only way to really "grab all the gusto" life offers! We simply mean put some spontaneity, some gusto, some zip into your life. Get off that diet of "vanilla," and get into these super flavors life offers.

Children have this "spark." They are born with it. Someone has said that true success is the ability to carry the genius of the child into manhood. For we are to grow out of childishness, but never out of childlikeness! Children still have the sense of "wonder." We should never lose it!

For your marriage, hug more and longer. Praise each other every day. Spend time alone together. It is too needed, too rewarding, not to do so. Hug your kids. Listen to their problems and their "discoveries." Don't miss out on the wonder of childhood; yours and theirs!

Drive home another way. Notice the trees, the hills, new construction. Notice and wonder! Smell the roses. Write "I love you" (and send it), hug your kids, say "I'm sorry," smile, go on a picnic, ride a roller coaster, watch a "Pink Panther" movie, read Proverbs, walk in the woods, talk to God with your eyes and heart open, take a vacation. Take one with just you and your wife; take another with the whole family. Don't always visit relatives. Go to Disneyland, Hawaii, go on a cruise, buy a water bed. Eat more ice cream! *But don't order vanilla!*

CHAPTER 10

NO ONE WANTS A PET BUZZARD!

THE world is "pet crazy." You've noticed that, haven't you!? And dogs and cats head the list. But from there we branch out to pet canaries, gerbils, hamsters, snakes, monkeys, kangaroos, turtles, ducks, crows, cows, and even "defumigated" skunks! And I'll lay odds, someone reading this book will say, "He left out mine!"

But no one wants a pet buzzard. People don't buy them; they don't want them in the house. They don't have pictures of buzzards on their walls. We don't even want stuffed ones! They are simply and emphatically obnoxious!

All that reminds me of the preacher who was doing a series of lectures in a distant town. He said to a young boy about five, "I'm supposed to go to your house for dinner tonight." The little fellow answered, "I know it!" "Well, what do you suppose we're having?" asked the preacher. "Buzzard," came the boy's firm reply. "Buzzard? Are you sure?" "Yep," said the boy, "I heard daddy talking about it. He said 'Well, if we've got to have the old buzzard, we'll have him for dinner tomorrow night.' " Needless to say, the preacher was not flattered!

People are a lot like animals. I'm sure you've noticed. One old spinster said, "Why do I need a husband? I've got a parrot that curses, a dog that sleeps all day, and a cat that stays out all night!" I've met a few men who fit that description.

We've heard it said, "He's like a big old teddy bear," or "he roars like a lion"; "he's mean as a snake," "stubborn as a mule." And you can fill in the rest! "Blind as a...," "eats like a...," "grouchy as a...," "sly as a...," "strong as an...." We also use, "he's crabby," or "his story is 'fishy' "!

But what is it about buzzards that no one wants them for a pet? And beware, because if you possess these traits, you'll be about as welcome as a skunk at a wedding, or a pork chop in a synagogue!

Buzzards look obnoxious from first glance. Their posture lends itself to a leaning, lurking appearance. Up close, they are dull and dirty, and the smell is awful. They circle in the air, looking for one thing. They want something dead or dying; something putrid and smelly! It is all they live for. They can spot "stink" a mile away, and hasten to the spot. If anything is sweet, alive and vibrant, you won't see a buzzard for miles around.

Some people, unfortunately, are too much like this. They want the "dirt," the scandal, the gossip. They are happiest when they know dark, dirty facts on other people, and delight in telling it to whoever will listen. Like vacuum cleaners, they pick up all the dirt they can find, but delight in dumping it into every conversation, no matter whom it hurts. This "buzzard quality" will earn you a reputation all right, but not many friends. Good people will avoid you like they do buzzards. They won't want to be around you.

And another thing, buzzards don't sing! If you want a singer, you look for a canary, or one of the many wild birds. You delight in having them around. They bring joy and happiness to everyone. There are both kinds of people. Some never sing. They never encourage. Nothing positive comes out of their mouth. Only the negative, the critical, the complaining. Then there are those people who bring their own sunshine with them wherever they go. Folks always feel better when they are around. They are cheerful, positive, excited, and exciting. They are natural encouragers! They listen, they notice, and they praise. Friends flock to the latter; and they run from the former. No one wants a pet buzzard!

Buzzards have a filthy appetite. They will find it under rocks and dark, out of the way places. They are like those people you see casting furtive glances around before they go into an "adult(?)" book store. They feed on pornography, which seasons their conversation with filthy, suggestive talk. They are anxious to hear or tell (more often, tell) the latest dirty joke. The more vulgar, the better! People hate buzzards for this reason; and a little bit of people like this goes a long way! You will not see a crowd of friends around folks like this. They may be a novelty, tolerated by a few, and for a short time. But long range friendships, and social success doesn't come to buzzards! We simply stay away from folks with "buzzard-breath!"

What are some of the traits of "buzzard personality?" Intimidation is one such trait! Some believe in "winning through intimidation." But those who "seem" to win in this manner find it a short success. In the long run, salesmen and others who follow the "intimidation" route will lose. Just here, I recommend for all salesmen Tony Alessandra's book, *Non-Manipulative Selling*. It is a classic. True salespersons help their customers get what the customer wants and needs. Such customers are glad, five years from the sale, that they bought. Salesperson and customer form a "friendship" that lasts beyond the business transaction.

Then there are the loud, obnoxious folks with "I" trouble. "I" did this, and "I" did that; tooting their own horn! Some do all the talking; they've always got to "out-do" you. If you caught a fish, they've caught a bigger one. If you landed a sale, they've landed a bigger one. They can never be content just listening and congratulating. They must play "one-up-man-ship" constantly! And they do so at a loss of good friends.

Others are the "know-it-all's," the gossipers, sometimes known as "hoof-and-mouth disease" (they "hoof" it over to their neighbors and "mouth" off)! Following this are the grouchy, the critical, the complainers who love to "garbage dump" on all they meet. They smother you with their troubles. It reminds me of Cavett Robert's line, "Don't tell other people your problems; 80% don't care, and the other 20% are glad it happened to you."

Then there are the negative thinkers, the broadcasters of "gloom and doom," full of whining and self-pity. Add to this the "takers," and this about rounds out "buzzard personality." Simply put, "no one wants a pet buzzard!"

Well, what does it take to have friends? Lots of friends; good friends, friends for a healthy, life-long relationship? We might take another look at animals. Why do people like the pets they have?

Well, they like dogs because of their loyalty; their faithfulness. Someone said, "they wag their tails and not their tongues." There's probably some truth in that. They like cats because they are cuddly, and want affection from you. They like canaries because they are bright and sing beautifully. Things like "soft, cuddly, friendly" are the reasons most people pick the pets they have. They like the same things in people.

I asked my "Peak of the Week" class what they liked in their friends. Here are some of their answers: "sincerity, confidentiality, positive attitude, cheerful, loyal, can relax around them, they let you be 'you,' accepting, they are givers, lovers."

Do you realize this is exactly the kind of person the Bible instructs you to be? And there are so many people who fight the Bible, God and church, somehow believing it isn't the "normal" way to live. All God wants is for you to be happy, healthy, prosperous, and have lots of friends. In short, what the world wants in friends are the people living like the Bible says. You'd think we'd catch on!

If you were not "you," would you want you for a friend? Wow, that's a tongue-twister! Read that again! It says simply, would you want someone like you as a friend. If not, don't be surprised if you have few friends. Concentrate on developing in yourself those qualities you'd want in a friend. It's a pretty sure thing that in no time at all you'll have all the friends you need.

Being a friend, and having friends is entirely within your grasp. Just remember, "no one wants a pet buzzard!"

CHAPTER 11

FOOL THINGS I'VE DONE

DO you ever do "fool things?" You know, those things you do, and you hope nobody finds out. You pull some stupid stunt and immediately look all around so sure there are a million people standing there, laughing at what a miserable thing you just did! I do things like that regularly!

The other day I walked into my "Auto-bank." I pulled a card from my wallet and inserted it into the slot. The machine responded with "please enter code again." Thinking I had transposed the numbers I made a fast correction, and the machine kept my card...and the steel window dropped. I grabbed the red telephone (thinking it might contact me with the President of the United States).

"Your machine ate my card," I said frantically. The lady on the other end of the phone said, "Mr. Phillips, read me the numbers across the top of the form the machine gave you." I read her this long, 12-digit number. There was a pause! Then she said, "Mr. Phillips, you inserted your Mastercard, instead of your Transfund card." She explained nicely that my Mastercard would be returned in the mail; and that I should now insert the proper card, and I could get the transaction I wanted.

I looked all around. I was to speak that night to my "Peak of the Week Class" on "Fool Things I've Done"! My list had just grown longer.

I keep two boxes. One is my "Good Memories Box." I put in little cards, and those special letters from people who thank me for blessing their lives. It is a needed box. Every now and then, when things aren't going well, when I wonder if I really am a help to anyone, I can look in that box, and it restores my self worth.

But the other box is my "Fool Things I've Done Box." I also keep a record of things like the above mentioned fiasco at the Auto Bank. It keeps my sense of humor; it helps with the balance between egotism and depression.

We all act the fool now and then. Even Samuel in the Bible said, "Surely, I have acted like a fool and have erred greatly" (1 Sam. 26:21).

It is said that Edward M. Stanton, Lincoln's war secretary, once refused to carry out a presidential order. And he was said to have called Abraham Lincoln a "fool" for having issued such an order. Lincoln issued the classic reply, "If Stanton said I'm a fool, then I must be; for he is nearly always right. I'll just step over and see for myself." And Stanton convinced him to change the order.

It was reported that Benjamin Franklin had taken a personal inventory and wrote down thirteen faults he thought he had. He put them in a list and battled them one at a time. He'd take them on, one each day. And he kept records of who he thought won the battle that day. And he kept it up for more than two years. No wonder he was such a well-loved man.

So we all do fool things. What sets us apart is the ability to see them and to respond the right way to the fool things we've done! Here are a few of mine!

"I've blamed my troubles on other people!" It's so easy to say, "Look what you made me do!" It is far easier to blame others than to apologize and take the blame for your own behavior. In the Garden of Eden Adam said, "The woman you gave me...SHE beguiled me, and I ate." It is true Eve sinned and equally true she offered the fruit to Adam. But from there on it was Adam's show! He could

refuse or accept; he chose to accept and made matters worse by blaming the woman. People have been doing it ever since. In 1 Samuel 15, the Prophet Samuel accused King Saul of disobeying God in the battle against the Amalekites. King Saul's answer? "The people wanted to do it...*they*...!" Well, the people were punished, but so was King Saul, for we are accountable both for what we do, and what we allow! And while I'm in the Bible, we should read Gal. 6:5 where the good book says, "Every man shall bear his own burden!" It is a mistake to blame your troubles and mistakes on other people.

"I've let other people's problems affect me!" Zig Ziglar does a marvelous job telling about the executive who was trying to get all his employees more punctual! He said, "We've been getting here late, and leaving early; we've been taking long lunch breaks. Now perhaps it has all been my fault. I'll shape up. And I expect you to follow my example!"

Well, he meant well. But a couple of weeks later he stayed too long at a lunch appointment and found himself very late. He knew they would all see him come in late. It would look very bad, especially after his "punctuality speech!" So, as he breezed in the door, he called out to his sales manager in a loud voice, "Meet me in my office. I want to know why you lost the Johnson account." Well, it diverted attention from the fact the boss was late. But it had a "ripple" effect! The sales manager steamed out of his boss's office. He immediately gave a rough time to his own secretary. She, in turn, lashed out at the receptionist at the telephones. It put the receptionist in such a bad mood, she went home, and took out her anger on her little son; who immediately left the room, and seeing his pet cat walking aimlessly into the room, gave the cat a kick saying, "Get out of here. You've probably been up to some mischief yourself." Ziglar's good advice, "Maybe someone has kicked his cat," is worth thinking about. It explains lots of behavior. We respond to others the way we've been treated ourselves. And it is a mistake! It is a "fool thing" to do. We have choice about our response. We can be happy "because of," or "in spite of" what has happened to us. Our attitudes are within our own power. If I choose to be happy, positive, and radiant, no one can change that attitude without my permission.

"I have talked when I should have listened!" Someone said, "Before you set your tongue in motion, be sure your mind is in gear." I haven't always done this. I have written letters in haste, and later regretted sending them. I have spoken harshly before I let a little time and rationality take control of my words. The Bible says, "He who answers before listening; that is his folly, that is his shame" (Prov. 18:13). Maybe that's why we have two ears, but only one mouth. Perhaps we'd all be better off if we listened about twice as much as we talk. I now make it a practice, with any letter about a touchy or sensitive theme, to write it, but not mail it for at least another full day. If at the end of that extra "think" time, I feel it should be mailed, then I do so. It has saved me a lot of pain and embarrassment!

"I have hesitated when I should have acted!" Sometimes I know full well what I ought to do. But I find a million excuses to put it off. And I am laden with "good intentions." I mean to go see that someone who is elderly and "shut in." I put it off too long. And then one day I get a call to come to their funeral. "Anyone, then, who knows the good he ought to do, and doesn't do it, sins" (James 4:17).

And speaking of funerals, there are always a lot of flowers around the casket. Somehow I keep thinking it would have been a lot better if those flowers had been given while the person was living. People make trips to the funeral, but through the years, "couldn't find time" to come enjoy a visit while that loved one was alive. It is a "fool thing" I've been guilty of that I'm determined to remedy. There are things that ought to be done now. Do a little thinking about this...and then act!

"I have worked when I should have taken off!" You know the opposite is true also. There are those so lazy,

you'd think they were in a contest for "laziness"; and they are sure to win! An employer of thousands was asked, "Just how many do you have working here?" and he answered, "About half of them!"

But while there is a time to get in there and work, there is also a time to "take off." I liked George Sheehan's article on "Giving the World Wednesdays Off." In it he suggested that on one day of the week, we ought to take it entirely for ourselves. No chores, no "honey-do," no "catching up!" Just do what you really want to do "for yourself!" That's when you'd smell the roses; watch a sunset; hold hands with your wife or sweetheart; do something with a child. Our national curse is "busy-ness." We are all going at break-neck speed, and really don't know what we've gotten accomplished when the day is done. We need time to catch our breaths, get a new perspective, regenerate the mind and body. Jesus said, "Come with me by yourselves to a quiet place and get some rest" (Mark 6:31).

"I've worried when I should have prayed!" You know, it's really foolish to worry and fret when you believe in God. He's in control; and He knows what He's doing! The Bible urges, "Cast all care upon Him; He cares for you" (1 Pet. 5:7). I saw a sign in front of a church, "Turn Care Into Prayer"! Boy, did I need that. People who worry, excessively, wear a sign for all to read, "I DON'T PRAY!". Jesus saw folks worried about food, clothing and shelter (Matt. 6:25-34) and He made them this promise, "Seek first the kingdom of God, and *all these things* will be given to you as well!" So it is a matter of priority and trust. Prayer will drive out worry, or vice-versa!

"I have listened to the wrong people!" You've really got to be selective about whom you listen to! Israel got into trouble with this a long time ago. Ten spies said they couldn't take the land God had given; two (Joshua and Caleb) said they could. The majority is not always right. Don't listen to negative thinkers. Watch those seven

"pall-bearer" words of any good enterprise, "We never did it that way before!" Maybe it's time we did!" Anyway, if we never try anything new, progress will halt in this generation.

"I have majored in minors!" My wife and I argued over some trivial something. Emotions went high, and I went for a drive to cool off. In the cool of the night air, I thought, "This is really silly. What we were arguing over was so small and insignificant!" I asked myself, "What *really is* important?" I reminded myself that my wife is a warm, loving and loyal woman. Her love and devotion to me is without question. Why should we be arguing about something so trivial? All of a sudden it didn't matter who was right; the issue itself wasn't all that important. I was "majoring in minors." I went home and told her I didn't care two figs about what we were discussing. From now on I was going to ask, "What really is important," and turn my attention to that! It has made a difference in our lives!

We often focus our attention on that which is insignificant. "Making a living" gets to be more important than "making a life!" We sacrifice love and compassion in order to "win"; to "come out on top." We allow the thoughtlessness of others to ruin our day. And "when we let little men cast long shadows, it is nearly sunset!"

Well, I think it will do you good to have a good look at the "fool things you've done." Laugh at them; learn from them! But remember, you'll never regret loving, giving, forgiving, serving, smiling and sharing.

So keep your "Good Memories Box"; and keep the box of "Fool Things I've Done." You'll learn from both; and both will do you good!

I just remembered; did I ever get my Mastercard back???

CHAPTER 12

YOU'RE NOT OLD
'TIL YOU'RE OLD!

I visited *Cornelia* the other day. It was her 91st birthday. I went back to her room, where she sat on the edge of her bed. She had on a pretty, bright dress. There was a lovely corsage on her left shoulder. Her lovely silver hair was arranged nicely, and there was a sparkle in her eyes. I got a hug and a kiss and wished her a "happy birthday." She was looking forward to a happy day, and there would be a party later in her honor, which she would enjoy.

Yogi Berra's statement came to mind, "The game's not over 'til it's over!" And I thought, "and you're not old till you're old!" Or maybe one I've heard Cavett Robert use; "Lord, don't let me die till I'm dead!"

Age Does Strange Things To People!

It reminds me of the spinster of 78 who died without marrying. She had stipulated in her instructions to her lawyer that there were to be no men pallbearers at her funeral...all women! Well, it was a strange request, since basically most pallbearers at funerals are men. But she explained, "Those rascals wouldn't take me out while I was alive; and they'll not take me out after I'm dead!"

How can you tell if you're getting old? I read a few pointers.

**Golfers can tell if they settle up after every hole.

**You're getting old, when someone at a party sets a glass of water in front of you, and you put your teeth into it.

Ann Landers added a few:

**When you still chase women, but have forgotten why!

**Your knees buckle, but your belt won't!

**You are 17 around the neck, 42 around the waist, and 126 around the golf course!

**You sink your teeth into a steak...and they stay there!

**You try to straighten the wrinkles in your socks; only to find out you aren't wearing socks!

I guess you're old when these lines fit:

"My bifocals fit,
My dentures are fine,
My hearing still works,
But I sure miss my mind!"

Well we have I.Q. (Intelligence Quotient) tests; even aptitude tests. Maybe we ought to come up with an A.Q. (Age Quotient) test! Consider the following:

**Does your conversation revolve around "Remember when" more than "I'm looking forward to"?

**Have you read any new books lately? (If you answer "why?" you're in trouble.)

**Do you have any goals for the near and distant future?

**Do you still express love?

**Are you involved in service to others?

Many people have a fear of getting old! To them "old age" denotes senility, uselessness, hopelessness and loneliness. It denotes decay, inability and inactivity. They feel they'll be "out of it," "on the shelf," "dependent," "over the hill!" And many people *are* old before their time. They become lazy, tired, dull, boring, critical and uncooperative. It is a strange paradox that we strive to retire young to do nothing; and then fear what that brings. We dread "pills, pain and-paralysis" (at least of ambition). But it doesn't have to be that way!

From the Bible, we consider several verses that show that God intends people to live long *and* happy!

"...fear God...keep His comands...that you may *enjoy* long life" (Deut. 6;2).

"...it is good and proper for man to find satisfaction.

"...God gives wealth and possessions, and enables him to enjoy them, to accept his lot, to be happy in his work; this is a gift of God...reflect on the days of his life, God keeps him occupied with gladness of heart" (Eccl. 5:18-20).

"However many years a man may live, let him enjoy them all" (Eccl. 11:8).

The greatest thing you can learn about God is that He is your Father. Now what do fathers want? I'm a father! I know what I like for our three kids, even now that they are grown and married. I want health, wealth, and happiness, both now and for eternity. And if God is your Father, He wants the same things for His kids.

It has been my pleasure to speak on several positive thinking rallies with Dr. Norman Vincent Peale. We have traveled some together. I remember once in Victoria, Texas, he said to me, "People shouldn't think *age*. Just concentrate on feeling good and attitude." Thinking age is bad for you. You'll always be saying things like, "I'm too old for that," or "a man of my age shouldn't be doing that." Or it can work the other way. You can always be worried about growing old, so you dress gawdy, buy ridiculous things, and try to disguise your years. At whatever age you are, you ought to think that's the best age there is. And if anything, feel a little sorry for those of any other age!

"You are what you IMAGE!" That's a favorite of Dr. Peale's!

Stay Alert And Active!

I scan the daily paper for good stories. I read of one, **Rose Blumkin**. She is 90 years old, buyer for her store, Nebraska Furniture Mart. She works 60 hours a week, has 500 employees and a $12 million annual payroll. Her philosophy is "sell cheap, tell the truth, don't cheat anybody and don't take kickbacks." Rose Blumkin is 90; but she's not old!
Irene is a member of our church. She is 80. She is a radiant person, and no one would guess she has lived 80 years. I buried her husband, Ray, last year. He was a happy, laughing, positive man. Irene follows the pattern. She sews like a professional. She made Ray's suits and shirts; she makes all the clothes she wears. She made me a beautiful white dress shirt. The tailoring is exquisite, and her own label adorns the inside of the collar, "Personally designed by Irene." She did not drive, but after Ray's death, she has bought a car and learned to drive. Someday she'll die, like all of us will, but she'll never be old.

Back to *Cornelia*. Although nearly blind, she cooks a hearty meal once a week for her grown grandsons who run an oil company nearby. She insists on doing all the cooking and washing all the dishes afterward. "You're not old till you're old!"

How To Live Long Without Getting Old

We all want to live a long time. We just fear getting sick, getting crotchety, senile and dependent. What's the best way to live long and still have a vibrant, happy life?

Accept your age as the best age! What should a person of your age be doing? The answer is "anything you want to do! Anything you choose to do!"

Think positive and active! The Bible says, "As a man thinks in his heart, so is he" (Prov. 23:7). It's like we say in computer language, "G.I.G.O." (Garbage in—garbage out). Whatever you put into a computer is what you get out. The same is true of your mind. "Your life becomes what your mind is fed!" If you feed it "old thought," negative and dull feelings, that's the way your mind and body will react. But if you feed it the good, the positive and the powerful, your life will come out that way.

Live in the NOW! One fellow said, "I'm not interested in a 'has-beener' or a 'gonna-be-er'; I want an 'is-er'!" Don't live in the regretful past, or even the pleasant past. "Yesterday is a cancelled check; tomorrow is a promisory note; today is the only cash you have...spend it wisely." Recovered alcoholics have learned to live "one day at a time." Grab today, and go for the "gusto!"

Take part in LIFE! Attitude is just about everything. Grow, learn, improve, change. This is a "changing world." You've got to stay up, or lose out! Be a participator, not a spectator. Get out in nature. Get among the azaleas, the dogwoods; hike, jog, bike! I share Dr. Leo Buscaglia's love of leaves. There ought to be a law against raking leaves. Leaves are to walk through, kick, throw, roll in, cover up each other in...or simply to watch! Enroll in a running club, watch funny movies (my favorites are the Pink Panther ones). Serve others. Stay vibrant, believing, alert and in touch. Keep a boundless faith in God, your country, your fellowman, and above all in yourself!

Does any of this make sense? Of course it does, because "You're never really old...till you're old!"

CHAPTER 13

YOUR
BEAUTIFUL BODY!

IMAGINE you are a senior in high school! It is graduation week and the gifts start coming in. There are the usual watches, ties, socks, books and assorted paraphernalia. But Mom and Dad have that "gleam" in their eyes. They tell you how proud they are of you. There are tears in their eyes. And they lead you outside. And there parked in the driveway is the most beautiful sports car you've ever seen. You've dreamed about having one like it. It is the color you wanted, with all the accessories you ever imagined. They hand you the keys. This is your graduation present! Thrilling isn't it?

Well you got such a gift at birth. Your Father (God) gave you a fantastic sports car more exquisite and expensive than any made on earth. It is your body; your beautiful, human body!

What? Me, beautiful? Shoot, I just looked in the mirror this morning. My nose is too big. One of my ear lobes is longer than the other one. My eyes are too close together. My hair looks like a mop. I'm too fat...too thin...too tall...too short.

Hold it! Somebody has done a job on us. Our modern world has us all believing you've got to be a certain size, shape, height and weight to be *normal*. Tell me, who wrote the book on *normal*? I'll tell you what normal is. Normal is a man, 5'9", 160 pounds, grey hair, and little "love handles" around the middle. Too bad about the rest of you. I'm tired of some "unauthorized idiot" writing his own book about normal and laying a trip on me.

I speak before thousands each year. Audiences of several thousand in rallies and workshops around the country. National conventions of large companies; sales seminars for various kinds of products. And of course, church groups from coast to coast. I see a lot of people. And you know, all I see are "beautiful bodies." Folks with the bodies God gave them; and you know, He never made any junk.

Oh, I see folks who don't take care of those bodies. And that's a shame. But beautiful bodies are what we've got. Let's learn to appreciate them, take care of them, and praise God for them!

The Real "You"!

Cosmetics are great, you know! But they've been misused, because some folks won't be seen without them. They've been brainwashed to believe they are unacceptable without painting and covering up. I'll be the first to confess that any old barn looks better with a little paint on it, but people are lovable, "warts and all." That new sports car will look better if it is washed and polished. But it is a fantastic machine even if it is dirty. Are you catching on?

You've been made in the image of God. Our earth is in an unfathomable galaxy. Scientists tell us our galaxy is one of millions of other galaxies. Just on our earth, there are millions of species of animals and plants. There are so many kinds of metals and minerals. But *you* are the only thing created in the image of God. Humans, alone, have a touch of "Immortality!" Pretty fancy stuff!

In the Psalms, David said, "I praise you, for I am fearfully and wonderfully made" (Ps. 139:14). David realized he had a beautiful body. And he only knew a fraction of what you know today. Just think! Isn't the human body something?

Many years ago someone invented a camera. It was a big box looking thing. The photographer had to put a black sheet over his head. There was a chemical flash, and a black and white picture resulted. The slightest movement caused a fuzzy, out of focus picture. We've come a long way, baby. Now we've got cameras that develop right before your eyes, all color, focused and ready to handle.

But God put a camera in the first man He made. It was instant, self-focusing, self-developing, all color. It was even self-repairing. It was the human eye.

A hundred years ago, the telegraph was invented. And man could send messages through little wires, and communicate over long distances. Everyone thought this was really something. And it was.

But God put a telegraph system in Adam. When Adam stepped on a sharp rock, little messages traveled through the nerves to the brain, "Ouch! It hurts down here!" And the brain would respond with "well, get your foot off that rock, you fool!" And every human has these and other sophisticated processes. We really have a remarkable, beautiful body!

The body is self-repairing. The skin, organs, all the systems (cardiovascular, respiratory, digestive) all cooperate together in a way that boggles the mind. And the best way to preserve it all is to relax, obey the rules and enjoy your "fabulous sports car" body!

Preventive Maintenance!

Our problem today is that folks don't realize just how sophisticated this body is, and we abuse it. It must have care and protection, just like an automobile. With a car, if you use the wrong gas, neglect to change the oil and filters, you'll end up with trouble. The body is the same. **Ken Cooper** says, "We do not die, as much as we kill ourselves".

Your body comes with a warranty of about 75 years. Take

extra good care of it, and it will probably serve you for many more years. Less care, less years! It is more within our own choice, than that of accident, disease or circumstances. The ages of 35-54 are the prime ages of "unnecessary, preventable death". You need to watch your blood pressure. Don't let it remain over 140/90. This is affected by diet, salt intake, weight, tobacco and exercise. All of these are "controllable". Alcohol abuse is responsible for 90% of deaths from cirrhosis of the liver. Tobacco is responsible for a third of a million deaths per year through lung cancer, enphysema, bronchitis and heart disease.

Feed that beautiful body right! This will not be a study in nutrition, but I will give these general rules for food, exercise and relaxation:

1. Get the right kind.
2. Avoid the wrong kind.
3. You can't get all you need at one sitting.
4. A steady, regular, consistent program works best.

Concerning diets, avoid the "crash diets". You will lose pounds, but your metabolism will also drop. Then you'll gain more weight on the same amount of food you ate before. Dr. Cooper recommends about 2000 calories per day, 30 aerobic points of exercise per week, and 8 hours of sleep per night.

Exercise

We must say a word about "aerobics". This means any exercise where you get the heart rate up to 120-150 beats per minute, and you sustain it for about 20 minutes. You should do this with approval from your doctor. But it has "roto-rooter" affect on your arteries. One who does this is not a likely candidate for "heart bypass" surgery. Exercises that are good for this include jogging, walking, bicycling, mountain climbing, swimming, skating and maybe rhythmic aerobics or jazzercise.

Rest!

The apostles of Jesus had been so busy in their important work for Jesus. The Bible says "they didn't even have a chance to eat". And Jesus said, "... come with me, by yourselves, into a quiet place, and get some rest" (Mk. 6:31). As one of the nation's largest hamburger chains exclaims, "You deserve a break today". And you do! You need time off, vacations, a "change of pace". Stress is a killer. And to cope with it, you need to learn to rest, relax and enjoy re-creation! Take a walk by a creek; row a canoe on the lake. Take a cruise. Camp in the wilderness. It is good for the attitude. It will put you back together. You can use the increased energy for constructive projects.

All I'm saying is that God gave you that beautiful body. He wants you to really enjoy it. He wants you to use it to get all the blessings a Father wants His kids to have. One day you'll trade it in on an Eternal Model. Until then, take care of YOUR BEAUTIFUL BODY!

CHAPTER 14

"I NEVER KNEW YOU LIKED PIÑA COLADAS"

A few years back, Rupert Holmes did a song called "The Escape". The scenario was as follows. Their marriage had gone stale, like a worn out record. The zip was gone; flat was the word for it. He sat in bed reading the newspaper; she lay beside him fast asleep. And then, leaping out at him, was this ad in the "personals", "If you like pina coladas, getting caught in the rain, making love at midnight, in the dunes of the cape, etc. answer this ad, and we'll plan our escape".

Well the idea fairly set him on fire. Life was passing him by. He'd answer that ad. This gal was definitely for him. He glanced over at "sleeping ugly". Yes, she was for him all right. He responded to the ad. He liked all those things. She was his type all right. They'd meet at O'Malley's and plan their escape.

He got there first. He had high hopes. She walked in. And he realized in a moment it was his own wife. They laughed for a moment, and then he said, "I never knew you liked pina coladas" etc.

There is sadness, pathos in that song. It haunts me. They'd been married 20 years, yet they really didn't know each other at all. Their interests led them to this "escape"; they didn't know they had so much in common.

WHY DIDN'T HE KNOW?

This Is The Age Of Knowing!

Never before has our world had so much technology, so much knowledge about *everything*. This is the age of "specialization"! We've got schools, courses, books, research and computors! We know who our ancestors are... but don't know where our kids were last night. We know our jobs; we know songs, singers; movies and movie stars. We score high on "Trivial Pursuit", but don't realize life is not a "TRIVIAL PURSUIT"! Many husbands know the facts of life, but don't know the "facts of *wife*"! The man in the song knew all about his wife...yet he knew nothing about her at all.

Husbands, take this quiz: When is your wife's birthday? How old is she? What is her dress size? Her shoe size? Ring size? When is your anniversary? What is her favorite food? Color? What are her views about kids? school? clothes? sex? church? you??? What makes her happy? sad? mad? loving? irritates? When did you last take her out? Would she like "making love at midnight in the dunes of the cape?"

And wives could take a similar test!

Is It Really Important To Know?

It is important to know only if you want to be happy! Otherwise it doesn't matter. If you want to be healthy, wealthy, and satisfied, then it's important. If success, achievement, love and salvation are important, then it's important to know.

Communicating is so important, deaf folks come up with sign language. Its importance exacted the inventions of the telephone, telegraph, TV, radio, newspapers, magazine, satellites and morse code.

Somewhere I read the story of Captain Gerald Coffee, who was a POW in Hanoi, North Viet Nam. Prisoners developed a code system to communicate with one another. It was essential to their sanity. They developed a simple 25 letter alphabet (leaving out the letter "K"). They stacked them in rows of five. They tapped, first for the row then for the letters. For example one tap, a pause, followed by two taps would be the letter "B" (first row, second letter). When the Viet Cong became suspicious, they disguised with coughs and wheezes for pauses, mop noises, wood chopping etc. for taps. One newly captured inmate learned the code. It sounded like the wheezing and coughing and bumping of a dying man. But all he was doing was conveying, "Miami Dolphins made it to the Super Bowl". They memorized the names of other prisoners, their families' names. They daily joined in the "Pledge" and the 23rd Psalm. Why this elaborate dangerous communicating? It is important to know, and to share!

Meanwhile, back in America, in many of my audiences, with so many ways to communicate and share, to KNOW ABOUT ONE ANOTHER, we stay at arms length, and become total strangers to the ones we love most. We can "say it with flowers"; you can use Hallmark, "when you care enough to give the best"; you can "reach out and touch someone" by telephone. You can look them in the eye and say, "I love you"! And no obstacle but pride, busy-ness, and selfishness stands in our way. We do "know" and we "can respond". Why then, those sad words, "I never knew..."!?

There's Too Much "I Never Knew"!

Most problems are communication problems. It is a matter of "I never knew", but "I could have known"! In business we are "product wise, but people poor". Never have our salesmen known more about their products than now. But many know nothing about their customers. And "folks don't care how much you know, until they know how much you care"!

It holds true in marriage. Families spend time "beside each other", eyes toward the "tube", never looking at each other, never sharing hurts, dreams or ideas. And if the TV fails, we might have to get acquainted all over again. It takes time, energy, effort, study to KNOW. There must be desire, interest and listening. It takes apology, correcting mistakes, repeating and giving benefit of doubt if you COME TO KNOW! But it is infinitely worth it!

Well, the song worked out. After the rendezvous the husband and wife of the "Pina Colada" song, were delighted to find out they were in fact, what each other really wanted and needed. And they planned their escape. They went out to do some of those crazy, fantasy things they'd dreamed about. It's the only thing that makes the song redeemable. And I hope that you and your "loved ones" will really come to know each other... and you can escape your heartache, and emptiness, into happiness and meaning...TOGETHER!

CHAPTER 15

CLOUDS!

CLOUDS are beautiful things! Floating up there in the sky. They're nice to look at, just laying on your back on a warm summer day! That reminds me of the characters of the comic strip, "Peanuts". They were doing just that! Laying out there in that triangular fashion; Lucy, Schroeder and of course, Charlie Brown. Lucy remarked, "Oh, just look at those clouds. I think I see Washington on the Potomac, leading all his men". Schroeder chipped in, "I think I see Beethoven conducting his fifth symphony". Lucy said, "What do you see, Charlie Brown?" And Charlie remarked in typical fashion, "I was going to say I saw a ducky and a horsey, but I...".

Clouds make nice pictures. We say, "she's got her head in the clouds". We fantasize about angels floating around on clouds, plucking their harps. Clouds!

The Bible says a lot about clouds. God appeared to Moses in a cloud. A cloud led Israel from Egypt to Canaan. It was a cloud that received Jesus back to heaven after his resurrection. The Bible further says that Jesus is coming again in the clouds; and that Christians will rise to meet the Lord in the clouds, "and ever be with the Lord". Clouds!

But to pilots, clouds are a menace! Especially in light aircraft. I remember flying to a speaking engagement in a small private plane, with three friends. The clouds were thick.

It was stormy. That plane pitched and tossed like no other plane in which I've flown. There were some uneasy moments. Clouds are not always seen as nice fluffy bits of cotton against a blue sky! I flew over the Bass Strait in Australia in a commercial aircraft. Clouds obscured sight; lightning flashed. The plane hit airpockets that literally lifted us off our seats. At times like that, you do not look on clouds with favor. One of our fine preachers, president of a school of preaching, along with three of his staff were lost in the clouds. They didn't realize how close to the ground they were; they hit some trees. And every man aboard was killed!

Clouds are full of thunder, lightning and turbulence. They cause airplanes to pitch and fall. No one ever wants to go up and just fly around in the clouds.

And I guarantee your life will have clouds. You can no more avoid turbulence in *life* than you can clouds in the sky! They are there as an undisputed fact. You may say, "I don't want any clouds in my life". But they are coming. Of that you may be sure. And it is not even in our best interest to *not* have them!

There will be clouds of pain and anxiety. Clouds of sickness and separation will come. Some experience the horrible clouds of divorce, or death of a mate. There are clouds of family stress, and financial loss. Accidents we did not expect, come as clouds giving severe turbulence to our lives. Other clouds such as disappointment, bitterness, loneliness and jealousy cause painful times in our lives. One way or another, clouds will assault your peace. You will be shaken, and sometimes cannot see the way. And some days you will be unable to see any blue or sun at all!

The Value Of Clouds

Is there any value in clouds at all? Would life be better if we could rid ourselves of clouds once and for all? And would life be better if we could eliminate all our problems?

Remember it is from clouds that the earth gets its needed

rain. And it is the contrast that makes beauty. It is like the guy who was asked, "How's your wife?", and he replied, "Compared to what?"! It is all "compared to what?"!

I spoke to a singles' seminar recently. They were a lovely and warm audience. My heart went out to them. But they've all suffered the loss of a marriage, one way or another. My life is absolutely perfect compared to that of a broken home.

Remember the guy who died in the Johnstown flood? He went to Heaven all right. And on "show and tell" day, he longed to tell the story of the Johnstown flood. Saint Peter finally said it would be all right, but perhaps he should remember that Noah was in the audience. One preacher had a sermon title, "Don't Tell Your Flood Story to Noah". It simply means that a little looking around, and maybe our clouds aren't so bad after all by comparison!

Clouds make you stronger. Tell me the truth, it you're going flying someday, would you rather have a pilot who'd been through a few clouds, or one who had successfully avoided ever having that experience? It is victory over adversity that brings strength. Body builders do not develop muscles lifting powder puffs. Some of the most beautiful coral in the world is found on the Barrier Reef in Australia. But in the cove, the coral is beautiful in shape and color on the ocean side; but white and shapeless on the protected side. The difference is struggle. The coral that endured the battering of the waves was made more beautiful in the struggle. Isn't there a lesson in there somewhere?

And clouds make you appreciate the "blue skies" more. A clear blue sky is more magnificent after a storm. And I have witnessed a much sweeter spirit, more expressed love in the Garnett Family after we have gone through some bad times. Storms make unity and peace sweeter. And never forget clouds are what make rainbows!

How then do we handle our "clouds"? First of all, understand clouds are inevitable. Therefore "accept" them. We fret less, when we understand clouds are as natural as the blue sky. Second, don't give in to them. A pilot in a storm who throws up his hands and quits, is going to crash. Resist them, learn from them, resolve to overcome them. You'll be out in the blue again in no time. Last of all, keep going "up"! Pilots know when in the clouds, that if they keep going up, they'll soon be out of them. There are all kinds of "looks". There is the backward look, the forward look; even the inward look. But it is the *"Upward look"* that brings us out of the clouds and to victory.

After the flood during Noah's day, God put a rainbow in the clouds. It was His promise never to destroy the world by water again. And if you'll let Him, He'll put a rainbow in your clouds today!

CHAPTER 16

YOUR FACE AFTER FORTY IS YOUR OWN FAULT!

CINDY Cochran is a dear friend of mine. She has her own television show in Houston, Texas, and is a positive, dynamic speaker and lady. Her stock answer when someone says, "This is just not my day", is "Well, whose day is it, then?" It makes a good point.

So many people go through life complaining and griping! It is the source of much stress. And it results in failure, depression and loneliness. For who wants to hang about a "Rain cloud", or an "accident waiting to happen"?

And "blaming" is a wonderful escape! "I came from a broken home". "My father left me when I was little"; "We were very poor"; "I belong to a minority group". All this "excusing" began when Adam said to God, "The woman *YOU* gave me is the problem"! Please recall Adam didn't get away with it. And neither will you. We are so much more in control of our destinies than many believe. My message to you is "your face after forty, is your own fault".

You Are Not Responsible For The Face You Were Born With!

Ending a sentence with "with" reminds me of a fellow who showed up for a meeting of a very sophisticated and exclusive club. "Where is the meeting at?", he asked. He was told rather curtly, "You do not end a sentence with 'at'". To which he replied, "Okay, where is the meeting at...TURKEY?". Sometimes we'd better leave well enough alone!

Anyway, where was I? Oh, yes! Your past *explains* you; but it doesn't lock you in! It is sometimes amusing to hear people bragging about being from a certain state. Or who their parents were. Or maybe about being white; or black. Friend, you can't take credit for the state in which you were born, or the parents God gave you, any more than you can take credit for the face you got at birth!

It reminds me of the little black boy who watched the balloon man at the circus. Every now and then he would release a balloon and as it would fly upward folks would notice, gather around and buy balloons. He released a yellow one, and then a red one. Then a white one. Finally the little fellow asked the man, "Mister, if you let a black one go, would it fly as high?" The wise old balloon man said, "Son, it isn't the color of the balloon that makes it go high; but what's on the inside". We all get the point!

It has been my privilege on several occasions to share the platform with the great Art Linkletter. I have heard countless times his story about being left, as an abandoned child, on the doorstep of a penniless Baptist preacher in Moose Jaw, Saskatchewan Canada. What if he had been found instead by John D. Rockefeller, who often hunted in that area? Who were his real parents? And what might he have become if his early start in life had been better? Would any dare to say, that this "living legend" (as he has been called) might have done more, made more money, contributed more to society if he had had more to start with? It isn't where you came from, neighbor, or your heritage; as much as "what are you doing with what you've got?"

Choice And Training!

There simply is no pattern for success. It isn't a

matter of age, race, or heritage. And the rules for success are "identifiable" and "learnable". You can find the factors that made others succeed, and the good news is you can also do it!

Randy was a senior in high school. He was a good football player. He might likely get a scholarship from college. This would pay college expenses, and who knows, he might end up earning millions in professional football. But in an accident on his summer job, he lost an arm. Folks couldn't get over how well he coped with this tragedy. He explained it was the wisdom of his father who told him simply, "you can't worry about what you've lost; you've got to concentrate on what you've got left"! Good advice. And it is too soon to trace the success of this young man. But with an attitude like that, you can believe he'll be a success!

She was 38, broke, a scrub woman with no future. Or so it seemed. But she read Claude Bristol's book "The Magic of Believing", and it turned her thinking around. Phyllis Diller now commands fame and fortune in the entertainment world. What life has dealt you at birth is one thing; but your face after forty is your own fault!

The great Milton overcame his blindness. Beethoven composed some of his best works after going deaf. Franklin Delano Roosevelt will always be known as the only man ever in history to campaign successfully for the Presidency of the United States *four consecutive times.* Yet he did this from a wheelchair; for he was the victim of the crippling disease, polio! It isn't the number, or even the size of your problems, but what you do about them that counts!

Somewhere I read the lines,
"I had the blues because I had no shoes,
Until one day upon the street,
I met a man who had no feet".

To Get More, You Must Produce More!

While I was serving with the USAF in Korea, I saw a

training film in a leadership course entitled, "To Get More, You Must Produce More". It was a classic. It explained a simple, basic law for "getting", "growing", "succeeding" that comes from three, rather simple Bible verses.

Luke 6:38 reads, "Give, and it will be given to you. A good measure, pressed down, shaken together and running over, will be poured into your lap. For with the measure you use, it will be measured to you".

The problem with that verse is our "church use" of it! Preachers jump us, quote the verse, and send the collection trays down the aisles. You may notice that "money" is not mentioned in that verse. Nor is it mentioned in the entire chapter. I'm sure money is "included", but "money" is not the subject. It is a principle of life. The "it" applies to anything, bad or good. If you want *trouble,* give it; you'll get plenty of it in return. But suppose you want smiles, prosperity, friends, success in your business, marriage or church? The more you give, the more you're going to receive.

Jesus told his disciples, "whoever wants to be great among you, must become your servant" (Matt. 20:26). Again, in a religious setting we stumble over this. While Avis (or whoever tries harder), Marriott Hotel Chain, General Motors and others use this principle to build great businesses and accumulate fortunes.

Positive thinking speakers coin a phrase from this verse. It goes, "You can get anything in life you want, if you just help enough other people get what they want"! It is working every day. All around us. And when we realize it, we can put it to work for ourselves. Put another way, "We've been dealt certain cards in life, but how we play them is up to us". Put another way, "Your face after forty is your own fault".

There are three laws of sowing and reaping, as again found in the Bible. "A man reaps what he sows" (Gal. 6:7). The three laws are as follows:

You reap *what* you sow!
You reap *more* than you sow!
You reap *later* than you sow!
And these are *"laws"*, not theories or possibilities! When applied to selling, or to life itself, these laws can help you build your dreams to reality!

Final Applications!

Now let's get personal, here at the end of this chapter on "Your face after forty is your own fault". Let's apply this first of all to your appearance! It is remarkable today what can be done with cosmetics, fashion, and fitness. And a beaming, radiant, positive attitude has its way of shining through the homeliest of features. So you really can be beautiful or handsome if you really make up your mind to be.

And then there's emotional stability. Don't tell me about your childhood. It would only *explain* you. It does not lock you in. Get a good grip on the philosophy "I'm OK; You're OK" (read the book by this title; it is a beauty). Read good books on self-image; Read God's book on self-image! Jesus thought you were worth dying for! Pretty valuable stuff, that's you!

And prosperity? You've lost it all? You are unskilled? You are past forty? Take a new look at the classifieds with belief in your own competence. Take a job at basic wage, but one where there is a future for one such as you who is willing to learn and be trained for leadership. The opportunities are unlimited for those who refuse to participate in the depression!

And what about "relationships" for those past forty? Damaged ones in the past don't have to stay that way. Swallow your pride. Muster the courage to get face to face and say "I'm sorry", "I love you", and "I was wrong". Maybe it was your fault back then. If it stays that way, it really will be your fault! You are only as rich as your relationships. Pay the price to have good ones!

And being a Christian, I am most interested in spirituality. The good news of the gospel is that no matter what you've done in the past, you can have a new start. Jesus Christ, the gospel of Christ, the church of Christ are all willing, even anxious, to help you get a brand new start. All we're saying is "if you get knocked down, that's bad! But if you *stay* down, that's your fault". For "your face after forty, is your own fault"!

CHAPTER 17

THE MASKS WE WEAR!

THE Tulsa World newspaper, Dec. 19, 1984, carried the letter. "Dear Ann," she wrote. And there followed a letter from a 16-year-old girl. She had a happy, carefree life, and wrote of a close friend who had just committed suicide. She said she seemed to have it all together and had a bright future. She couldn't work it out. Why would someone with such promise do such a thing?

It reminds us of the poem Ann also printed by Edward Arlington Robinson (1869-1935) entitled "Richard Cory."

> Whenever Richard Cory went downtown
> We people on the pavement looked at him,
> He was a gentleman from sole to crown,
> Clean favored, and imperially slim.
> And he was always quietly arrayed,
> And he was always human when he talked.
> But still he fluttered pulses when he said,
> "Good morning," and he glittered when he walked.
> And he was rich—yes, richer than a king,
> And admirably schooled in every grace,
> In fine, we thought he was everything,
> To make us wish that we were in his place
> So on we worked, and waited for the light,
> And went without the meat, and cursed the bread,
> And Richard Cory, one calm Summer night,
> Went home and put a bullet through his head.

The masks we wear! And we all wear masks. Oh, there are some we *should* wear. We don't want to "garbage dump" on other people every time we see them. When you ask that superficial question, "How are you?" you really don't want someone spending an hour telling you how bad they feel, and how gloomily they see the future. That will make you a "social leper" in a hurry.

But we wear other masks we could do without. We wear the mask of an "egomaniac." Some men wear the "macho" mask. One woman might enjoy the mask of "sultry temptress." We wear "tough" masks, and "don't care" masks; "I've got it all together" masks. Other masks identify us as "extroverts," "introverts," "nonchalant." Some masks are our silence; others are that we talk too much. Either way, down deep, is the real you, crying out to be discovered, accepted and loved!

Why do we wear all these masks? Why are we so afraid to let people know exactly who we are? Fear! That's it! We are so afraid so much of the time. We fear failure and rejection. We are afraid of death, the future, war, and a million other things. Fear drives us to wear our masks. One fellow said, "I used to have an inferiority complex. I went to a psychiatrist and I don't have that complex anymore. I found out I am inferior!"

But we're all alike. If we confessed all our fears, our weakness and mistakes to each other, we'd laugh at each other for our lack of *originality*. We are all just about alike. We all do stupid things, yet none of us are stupid. We are afraid we won't be accepted, loved and appreciated. Yet we are all lovable and capable. We all want to be open, sharing, enjoying, participating, contributing and helping. We all want to be a part of a loving group! Fearing we do not measure up, we adorn masks we think might help us be accepted.

There are some extreme tragedies that come from the masks we wear. A well known, well loved minister in Texas suddenly disappeared. When they found his car, there was evidence that he might have been robbed and kidnapped. A widespread manhunt ensued. There were reports that he had been seen here and there. Finally a private investigator was hired to trace down every lead. His conclusion was, that this man probably staged the whole situation; that he was alive and operating under his own power, and simply did not want to be found. He had a wife and family, and his church was totaly supportive of his ministry. Yet he apparently wanted to vanish into thin air.

What was behind those masks he wore? What problems and pressures that went unshared? What experiences that he could not communicate? One wonders what might have been different had he just taken off those masks to wife, church or counselor and worked toward a solution.

This brings to mind another bright young man I knew. He was one of the most effective youth ministers in the nation. Loved by thousands, yet one day he walked into his office, put a gun to his head and killed himself. The exterior read, "Hey, man, I'm OK. Everything is going fine." But it was a mask! There were clouds and storms going on inside this extremely valuable and talented man. He might yet be alive and working successfully among our nation's youth if he had shared what was behind all those masks.

We all tend to wear our masks. Most of us will not come to the tragic end portrayed in these two stories. But still our masks cost us. They keep reality out. They force a "played part" so that we never get acquainted with the warm, giving, normal person underneath. They create walls of separation and isolation. They keep folks from knowing what a wonderful person you really are.

There is a verse in the Bible (James 5:16) which instructs "Confess your faults, one to another, and pray one for another." Now this doesn't mean "tell everything you've done to everyone you meet." Disaster would come from this. Rather, I'll use the term "selective confession!" Find someone you can trust; someone who loves you and wants the best for you. If you have someone like this to whom you can share your heart, you are rich indeed! Someone said, "A friend is someone who knows all about you and loves you anyway!"

And this is the beautiful thing about God. He knows all about you and loves you anyway! God has seen everything you've ever done. He knows the reason you did it! He sees the motive behind the action! "All things are naked and open unto the eyes of Him with whom we have to do"(Heb. 4:13). That verse used to scare me to death. You've never fooled God in your life. But he sees you "warts and all" and loves you anyway! That must be what they mean by "grace!"

We all need to be accepted, forgiven, blamed, taken back, tolerated, given a second, third...even fiftieth chance! God gives all this. Praise him, we don't need our masks!

Let's make a few resolutions about our masks. Let's wear as few as possible. Experiment by taking a few of them off before trusted loved ones. Attempt getting them all off in front of God. Try to see behind the masks of others. Ask "Why?!" This will make you slower to blame people for their conduct. Maybe if the same things had happened to you, you'd wear the masks they wear!

Underneath all those masks we humans wear, live scared, lonely, lovable people. A man says to himself, "I'd love to ask her to dinner. But she would probably refuse, and I'd be so humiliated." The lady thinks to herself, "I wish he'd ask me out. I'm so lonely." So he doesn't ask. And they both lose!

The Bible says, "Jesus saw the multitude, that they were like sheep scattered abroad, having no shepherd. And He was moved with compassion" (Matt. 9:34-35). Oh, that we could see like Jesus saw. We see only the clothes, the hair, the flaw. Jesus saw their hearts and loved them. He sees behind the masks!

I close with a plea that you come out from hiding. A wonderful world of experiences and relationships awaits those who shed their masks, accept who they are, and pour their lives into others. And I urge you to look behind the masks of those you meet. Behind that harsh exterior, there is a person, created in the image of God, needing a friend like you. Things will take a turn for the terrific, when you decide to show the wonderful, lovable you hiding behind the masks we wear!

CHAPTER 18

"WHO TOUCHED ME?"

THE woman was completely unnoticed in the crowd. They were following Jesus. He was on his way to the house of Jairus, one of the synagogue rulers. His son was sick. Jesus had promised to heal him. It was a big crowd. But the woman noticed only Jesus. She had been bothered by internal bleeding for twelve years now. She had been under many doctors' care and spent all she had in medical bills. Her purpose was singular; "If I can just touch his clothes, I will be healed." She reached Jesus and took hold of his clothing. The Bible says, "Immediately her bleeding stopped" (Mark 5:29). But Jesus turned and said, "Who touched me?" (vs. 31).

Jesus was always touching folks. And they wanted to touch him. Jesus touched a leprous man (Matt. 8:3). There is more to this than meets the eye. People in Jesus' day were terrified of leprosy. It was demanded of a leper that if anyone came close, he was to cry out "unclean, unclean," so they would be warned away. There was great fear of it being contagious. But Jesus *touched* this leper!

And He touched two blind men (Matt. 9:29); "all who *touched* Him were healed" (Matt. 14:36). In the Garden, when a mob came to take Jesus for crucifixion, Peter cut off a man's ear. Jesus touched the man's ear, and restored it to its place (Luke 22:51). Jesus took little children in His arms (Mark chapters 9 and 10). "They all begged Him to let them touch Him" (Mark 6:56). Jesus was definitely a "toucher!" A telephone commercial says, "Reach out and touch someone." It is a nice and necessary thing.

There is this "distance phenomena" among we humans. We stand apart. We extend our hand briefly for a handshake and then quickly recover it. Get a few of us on an elevator together, and we don't know what to do about each other. We stand apart, eyes on the floor, glad to escape the closeness of other human beings.

My "Peak of the Week" class starts off with a "Hugger/Huggee" line. I ask for volunteer "huggers." They come stand beside me at the front of the room. I then give everyone in the audience two minutes to come through the line for a hug! We always have a wonderful time with this little ritual. The huggers and huggees alike seem to enjoy it to the full. But I'm constantly amazed that even in a setting like that, only about twenty, out of a class of over three hundred participate. And those sitting in the audience seem to enjoy it. (I wonder if "vicariously"?) I wonder why others don't race to that line to receive those wonderful, reassuring hugs. I wonder how badly the others need the touching tenderness such an experience gives?

Doctors and psychologists alike are speaking up today about the value of touch. The "Hug Club of Tulsa" visited our class one night, and sold T-shirts with their logo. On the back it says "12 hugs a day minimum." It just might be a much better world if everyone got a dozen sincere hugs from his fellowmen every day!

As badly as touch is needed, we might ask, "Why do we seem afraid to touch?" Fear of rejection would be one reason. Another would be that we connect touching to "flirting!" There are a couple of tragedies in marriage. One is that in sexual relationships between some married couples, there is not much tender hugging going on in the act itself. Also that outside of sex, not much other touching goes on between mates. Tragic, indeed!

So, touch who? And how? And when? Certainly touch your loved ones. Touch your mate, your kids, your friends and relatives. Give actual hugs, warm hand clasps, put a hand on their shoulder, hold tightly. When should I touch? When it is appropriate! And there are so many appropriate times. My weekly class gives an excellent appropriate time. Everyone knows we're going to do it. And many look forward to hugging, being hugged, or watching others get hugged! Hug when it is not expected. Hug apart from birthdays, when receiving gifts, or on your anniversary.

I preach for a large church. There are times when I'm completely surrounded by dozens of folks after my sermon. I'll feel someone lightly touch my shoulder, maybe even run that touch completely across by back. Many times I don't even know who it was. But I do so appreciate it. I enjoy the times we stand to sing "God's Family." It's become somewhat of a theme song for our church. Most always our people will stand, and join hands all across the auditorium. It is such a feeling of warmth and strength.

We bring lots of kids to church on our many church buses. Many of these children are never touched in love except when they ride our buses. Some are only touched when slapped, kicked or whipped at home. At first they hardly know how to respond when bus drivers, captains and workers, men and women, hug them, smile at them, and speak words of love to them. But they rapidly warm up to it. In no time at all, they want more.

And there are other ways of "touching" that include no physical contact. Smiles are really "non-touching" hugs! Compliments are "touch" in a very real sense. You ought to try to give at least three genuine compliments per day to folks you come in contact with. And then there are notes. My wife, Dot, is a notewriter. When I travel, I find them in my suitcase. There is always a warm note in every fresh shirt I put on. How do you think this makes me feel? Then there are "thank you grams!" Cards that say, "We're proud of you" or "Thank you." Hallmark has helped with beautiful and suitable verse when you "care enough to send the best." I read in the paper about a guy who rented a park bench which displayed a personal note to his wife. The sign changed each week. She drove past the bench each day on her way to her job. They've been on a perpetual honeymoon for many years now. He knows the value of touch!

Surprise loved ones, friends, workmates with little gifts, flowers, books, cards and praise. You'll find it pays far more than it costs!

So Jesus asked, "Who touched me?" And there's another kind of touch I want to discuss before we leave this chapter. The touch of influence! Our lives are changed and shaped as influenced by others. And likewise, others are changed by their contact with us. Like every hammer blow of a master sculptor, in both giving and receiving, we are shaped and being shaped by personal contact with others. That's why celebrities, professional athletes, politicians and other leaders need to watch their every word and deed. Someone is watching and will be influenced by everything you do. A British scientist estimated that nitrogen molecules are spread evenly all over the world; and that we've shared at least two of these molecules with everyone who has ever lived. Just think of it! You've shared the same air as Napolean, Abraham Lincoln, Cleopatra, Adolph Hitler, and Jesus Christ. We're not so far removed from each other, are we?

People are influenced by heredity. Heredity is just a touch of the past. Two generations down the line a child may come up as a mixture of Great Grandmother and Aunt Matilda. It may show itself in red hair, a way of laughing, walking and talking, or a dimple in the cheek. But we have been touched, and it explains so many things about us.

People of the past have influenced us. Institutions and inventions have influenced us. Just think how the automobile, the airplane and the television have affected our lives. Where would you be living today if not for Christopher Columbus? And you touch your children's lives by all you say, think and do.

This power of influence is so great. Jesus said, "Let your light shine before men; that they may see your good works and glorify your Father which is in Heaven" (Matt. 5:16). It is "touch" again working its way deeply into our lives.

So realize this power of touch. Use it wisely. A blind veteran was trying to make his way through the bus station to board a certain bus. A man, intending to help, grabbed him by the arm and said, "Come on, I'll see that you get on your bus." The blind soldier replied, "Don't push me. Don't possess me. I just need to feel the touch of your hand on my shoulder."

Folks today don't need to be possessed, pulled, dragged or driven. They just need the soft touch of our hand on their shoulder. Most of all, we need the "Touch of the Master's Hand." We're all in a crowd trying to find a safe place. Who touched me?

CHAPTER 19

THE DAY EVERYTHING WENT WRONG

DID you ever have a day when everything went wrong? And you said, "this is just not my day?" Well I had a day like that just a few weeks ago. And yet in the middle of the most trouble I've encountered in a long time, it was a fascinating day filled with many blessings. It taught me a great lesson. Looking back, I'm not sure I'd change anything about that day. Well, at least not *everything*!

It was Friday (not the 13th). Dot drove me to the airport for a 7 a.m. flight which would take me from Tulsa to Miami with an intermediate stop in St. Louis. Looking back now, I remember hearing about the passenger who said, "I knew we were in trouble when the pilot came on the intercom asking 'does anyone on board have a set of jumper cables?' "

There were three different flights on that trip. All three had trouble. First we sat on the ground in Tulsa for 40 minutes because of bad weather in St. Louis. Knowing we couldn't land in St. Louis, the pilot shut the engines off, and we just sat there on the runway until we knew we wouldn't have to circle the airport in St. Louis waiting for clearance to land. We circled anyway! That's when you realize you never saw one of those "trip insurance booths" in a bicycle shop. You never rode a train that had to circle the station for three hours.

I finally boarded the flight to Miami. But the plane had

radar trouble, and could not take off. They brought us back to the airport and finally suggested we board different airlines to our various destinations.

It was during this time, I saw him. He was an old man, sitting in a wheelchair, sort of staring at the floor. He was to be on my flight. I ended up sitting next to him on the flight that was never to take off. As the suggestion was made to change airlines, I found myself taking custody of this old man. And somehow, I also acquired custody of a Venezuelan lady and her daughter, neither of whom could speak English. The four of us had the same destination, and I guess I looked like I might be able to handle them.

His name was Eddie Adler. He was 95, in remarkable health, and an absolute joy to talk to. He has been about everywhere and done some fascinating things. I never saw him grope for words, or seem unable to remember some events, even though some of those experiences happened 75 years ago in his life. He was Jewish, and among the things we spoke about, we had a lovely talk about Jesus Christ. He was open, honest, and it was apparent we were becoming fast friends.

Just now, I need to expand on the troubles on these three flights, for these set up the great lessons I learned on that trip.

I speak very little Spanish. Just a few words I learned having grown up in San Antonio, Texas, which has a Mexican population of over 50 percent. Most of the words I learned would get my face slapped, so I carefully picked words for "gate number" and "time of departure"; and to reassure the ladies that everything was all right. It turned out they left hand baggage in St. Louis and thought I had stolen it. They thought Eddie and I were probably in cahoots; it was just a mess.

The final leg of my flight to Miami was so late, I had to go straight from the airport to the place where I was giving a marriage enrichment seminar. And my case of cassette albums, which would be offered at the seminar, did not come in on the same flight. The day everything went wrong...right? Wrong!

It was my friendship with Eddie Adler that redeemed the trip. Within a three-hour span we formed a deep friendship which remains intact today. I have written him and talked with him over the phone several times. I have extended him an invitation to visit our home in Tulsa.

Mit Schlamazel, Had Muir Glick

Shortly before we landed in Miami, this new-found friend of mine leaned over to me and said, "You know, Marvin, I feel we have become fast friends. I hope it doesn't end here. And I know we've had a lot of trouble on these flights, but it has been one of the happiest days of my life." And then he gave me this priceless bit of wisdom. He held up his left hand, which revealed two fingers missing. He said, "I remember when I got these fingers cut off in an accident. I ran crying to mother in panic. I remember that she held up the hand and said in relief, 'O thank God, you've still got your hand.'" And then my friend passed along to me the wisdom his mother gave him on that day. "Mit Schlamazel, Had Muir Glick...with all bad luck, also comes good luck" (roughly translated). There's lesson number one. In my case I had met this remarkable, lovely man, and we had become good friends. Our friendship would go on after we had forgotten all the other trouble.

I was late to Miami, but I did get to the seminar on time. It was a delightful experience. So nothing was lost. Even the cassette albums came the next day, and in the first seminar in my life, every one of them were sold. "Every cloud has a silver lining!"

Don't Sweat What You Can't Control!

I have no control over the weather, the radar on that airplane, schedule delays and changes. It is amazing how many people gripe and complain over these things and literally lose control of themselves. Their attitudes are shot, and their trip is "ruined" to hear them talk. Some don't see how they'll ever recover from what has "been done to them." It's almost as if the airlines has personally conspired to "do them in!"

I have a friend who flies internationally every year. Someone asked him if he worried much about crashing, since he was on so many planes, and traveled so many miles. His answer reaches me; "I never worry about what I can't control." You have complete freedom of dicision about *whether* to fly. But once you are in that plane and it takes off the ground, there is nothing more you can do to affect a safe landing. So trust the company that made the plane, the crew that serviced it, and the pilot who flies it. Only concern yourself about the things over which you have control.

You Can Stay In Control Of Your Day!

While you can't control other things, you can stay in control of your attitude and response. It isn't "what happens to you," but "what you *do* about what happens to you" that makes a difference in your life. No one can make you feel down, depressed, sad or negative without your permission. You have the choice to laugh or to cry at any event. People react differently to different situations. And it isn't simply because we are "different." Each of us has "choice." And we "choose" which way we want to react. Eddie and I chose to make the best of a bad situation. In the midst of bad weather, a radar that malfunctioned, transfer to an entirely different airline and flight schedule, we focused on the good things that were happening between us. We had formed a friendship, and I had learned bundles of wisdom from this dear old man.

Things Usually Turn Out Right If We Give Them Time

I found in most problem situations, if we just hang on, things will turn out all right. As I flew home from Miami, I reflected on the trip. What was lost by all the things that went wrong? I made it safely to Miami. I conducted a very successful seminar. I stayed with loved ones there. I met lots of lovely people. I sold all my cassette albums. And I landed safely back in Tulsa. Not one thing for which I made the trip was lost. It was a successful trip in every way. And as a bonus, I met Eddie and picked up some choice wisdom for life.

It's amazing how sometimes we feel that our problems are going to "do us in!" So many people feel that their problems are a "crisis from which they will never recover." In most, if not all, situations this is simply not true.

I'm a runner! Early in my running life I began to experience what runners call "stitches." These are little sharp pains that develop just above the belt line or in your back. You feel you can't go on. You breathe deeply, change your stride, wave your arms in an effort to get rid of the pain, and continue running. Most all runners understand perfectly what I'm saying.

One day I was reading a running publication. I came to a paragraph entitled, "What to do about stitches"! I thought, "Oh boy, here it is; information from the experts. I'm going to get a detailed analysis of the problem, a step-by-step solution." But here's the gist of all it said: "Accept them! No race was ever lost because of stitches. No one ever died because of stitches. The more you fight them the worse they feel. Relax. Just stay out there, doing what you're out there to do, in the most relaxed manner possible. And the stitch will go away."

Now, folks, it works in stitches. But it also works in life. We can fret and fight. We can stew and shout. But problems will always be with us. And situations will arise to threaten and send us into panic...if we let them. Relax! Keep your eyes on what you really want done. Keep at the task! Keep your eyes on the goal. Problems will come and go, but you'll get where you wanted to go in the first place.

YOUR FINAL DESTINATION

Tulsa was not in sight. The plane was descending. The pilot had assured us that we would be on the ground in Tulsa in about 10 minutes. And the flight attendant gave her final words over the intercom. "We hope you have a pleasant stay in Tulsa...or wherever your final destination happens to be."

Well, Tulsa is my home. And I was glad to get back there. Especially this time. But those last words somehow hung with me. "Wherever your final destination happens to be." I knew because of my faith in my Lord Jesus and the promises of His will that I really will have a fantastic time when I reach my *final* destination. And so will you!

CHAPTER 20

"LOVERS LIVE LONGER"

IT is usually when I'm in my pickup truck that I listen to country and western stations. I guess I'm living out the fantasy of the average American man. You know, blue jeans and cowboy hat, complete with boots. I've been thinking about getting a gun rack for the back window, and laying an arrow in it. And me, minister for one of the largest churches in the state. Ah, well!

At any rate, there I was cruising along the road, listening to KTFX, and the singer was belting out, "Lovers live longer...."

Now, I do a lot of talks on love. Looking back over the last year, I've done lessons in my "Peak of the Week" class on "Three Dimensional Love" (in this book), "Loving as a Way of Living," "Givers, Takers and Other Kinds of Lovers," and "We're Here to Love" (another country and western song).

And now this song with the philosophy that "Lovers Live Longer"! And I believe it is true. Our Handbook (the Bible) tells us so.

The word "love" takes up six columns in your Bible concordance (a book showing every word in the Bible in alphabetical order, and where it is used). Among these places are the following gems, "There remains three things; faith, hope and love. And the greatest of these is love" (1 Cor.

13:13). "Above all these virtues, put on love" (Col. 3:14). Then running your fingers through the "yellow pages" of the Bible you will find, "Love drives out fear" (1 John 4:18); "Whoever loves is born of God" (1 John 4:7); 'Whoever loves God must love his brother" (1 John 4:21). And when Jesus was asked what was the greatest command, He replied, "Love the Lord your God with all your heart and with all your soul and with all your mind. This is the first and greatest commandment. And the second is like it: Love your neighbor as yourself. All the Law and the Prophets hang on these two commandments" (Matt. 22:37-40).

God is a lover! "God is love" (1 John 4:8). "For God so loved the world" (John 3:16). And we are told there is nothing that can separate us from the love of God (Rom. 8:37-39).

But we naturally sense this. Most all our songs are love songs. They are about people in love, being unlucky in love, or looking for love. The theme of most books, movies, and even TV soaps is love. Love makes the world go around! We were designed to love and be loved. It is our nature. We sense this, and will do anything in the pursuit of love.

And you only get to keep love by giving it away. We sing a little chorus in Sunday School about,

"Love is like a shiny penny;
Hold it tight and you won't have any.
Give it away, and you'll have plenty.
You'll end up having more."

Love is a verb of action. It must have an object. And it must act. You cannot just "love"! You must love someone or something. And it must be expressed.

It needs to be expressed among our families. Husbands and wives must love each other. Not just because the Bible says so (and it does! Eph. 5:25), but because it is in our own best interest to do so. Husbands and wives need to express their love to each other. You do not tell your wife you love her to educate her. You do it to reassure her. And we all need reassurance. "When should you tell your wife you love her?" "Before someone else does it," came the reply!

And your kids. I pulled my truck into the parking lot at the Rose Bowl (bowling alley in Tulsa). "Well, have you?" yelled a kid sitting on the curb. I said, "Have I 'what'?" He pointed to my bumper sticker which read, "Have you hugged your kid today?" I said, "No, she's in college, but thanks for reminding me. I'll do it as soon as I see her!" I wondered what prompted that 10- or 12-year-old kid? Was he regularly hugged by his parents? I reminded myself to make sure I hug my kids, and my wife every time I have a chance.

The same goes for our parents, and our brothers and sisters. All too soon we gather around the casket of a departed mom or dad. Then, whether I have hugged them regularly becomes so important. Flowers for the dead are nice; but flowers, hugs, smiles for the living are so much more important. And loving, expressed, helps you live longer and better!

Extend this "loving" to other people. Love your fellowman. Love people in general. Extend it further to your job. "Love your job!" Wow, that's taking it a bit far, don't you think? No, I don't think so. In these days of job shortages and high unemployment, you have a great blessing if you have a job and make enough money to carry on your lifestyle. Be grateful and give it your best. You'll enjoy it more and live longer in the process.

And then love life itself. Give it lots of gusto...pizazz!! Get excited about opportunity and possibilities. Be thrilled with the potential there is out there for growth, achievement and success. Look with optimism to the future.

And then love the Lord as the "Great Benefactor" from Whom all blessings flow! Look at life as returning to the "Great Lover" your appreciation for all His goodness!

Express love with words. It would seem so easy to use words such as "I love you," "I appreciate you," "Thank you for what you did." But, alas, they are in short supply. These words bless the hearer. But more than that, they bless the "speaker." You'll be happier, healthier for the attitude behind those thoughts. Love with attitude! Let it show on your countenance; in your reaction and response! Express love with touch. Touching and affection are so necessary for health, wealth and happiness. Be thoughtful with gifts and remembrances. Add a warm note to the gift that says, "When I saw this, I thought of you." Be unselfish. Turn your interests to others. Thoughts turned inward cause the spirit to die. Turned outward and life blossoms and blooms and gives meaning to life.

The disciples asked Jesus, "Lord, teach us to pray!" Maybe we should ask God, "Teach us to love!" And prayer isn't a bad old place to start. God is your Father! You can ask fathers anything. They care! So ask God to fill your heart with love; to show you how to be a more loving and responsive person. Ask Him to teach you to be more like Jesus, the greatest lover of all time!

And then, expose yourself to love. It's hard to love people you are not around. You've got to get among people, associate with them, communicate with them if you are to love them. Decide to love. Love is more of a decision, than an inherited trait. Make up your mind you're going to be a lover. When Jesus commanded husbands "love your wives," (Eph. 5:25), it shows we can make up our minds about it. When Christians are instructed "Love one another with a pure heart fervently," (1 Pet. 1:22) it shows we have choice about it. You have choice about most everything. Decide to love!

And lastly, nurture love! Love is like a plant. Left alone without care, it withers and dies. Love needs constant caring and feeding. Do something every day to strengthen and grow love in your life. It will add to the quality and quantity of your years.

Why do lovers live longer? It is because they appreciate more, they stay in a better mood. Lovers have less stress, fewer ulcers, and less hypertension. Love is a valve that lets off steam and returns life to normal again. It is a hub to which all of life is connected. All the happy people are lovers! All the truly successful people are lovers. The only people going to heaven are lovers.

So eat right. Get plenty of exercise, rest and sunshine. Be careful crossing streets and learn to drive defensively. But most of all, learn to love; because "Lovers Live Longer!"

CHAPTER 21

THE PERSIMMON SECRET!

Remember the first time someone talked you into tasting a persimmon? That unusual looking, unusual tasting fruit, with so many little buds close together, and so many seeds? And how did it taste? Was it sweet or bitter? It all depends! And, wow, did you ever taste a green persimmon? It will pucker your mouth like alum. And do you know what determines if the persimmon is sweet or bitter? Different from any other fruit it *must* freeze to be sweet! Otherwise, it will be bitter. What would kill most fruits is a necessity to the persimmon. A good hard freeze while it is maturing will make it sweet, juicy and tasty! And so with us! How we handle adversity and crisis determines whether we will be sweet or bitter. We need to learn the persimmon secret!

It is a foregone conclusion that adversity will hit you. It is amazing how some people worry about future problems. They are afraid that problems will arise, or obstacles will come. Let me put your mind at rest. Problems will come! They will come to all of us. No one escapes hard knocks in life. Even the Bible says, "such things (adversity) must come" (Matt. 18:7). And again, "No temptation has seized you except what is common to man" (1 Cor. 10:13). We all have that "sin that so easily entangles us" (Heb. 12:1). So lust and greed are things we all fight. Accidents, sickness, financial reversal, failure, disappointment and trouble will come to all. Murphy's law, "what can go wrong, WILL," is proved again and again in all our lives. We are all alike in that we must attend the "school of hard knocks."

Nor is all of this bad! Adversity matures us! Obstacles strengthen us! The changing seasons of opportunity and adversity add color and challenge to our lives.

We subconsciously know this. And we even plan for them in the games we invent. Now you know they can plan a simpler golf course. We could play on a football field where the ground is level and there are no trees. Who needs lakes, sand traps and "dog legs to the right" anyway? If I designed a golf course, I would lay a pipe on the path between Tee and Hole, slanting downward. That way you'd make a "hole in one" every time. Isn't that the aim of the game? Or is it? And in football, I'd only let one team on the field at a time. How can you score a bunch of points when the other team has a "defensive team" in the game? And their precise aim is to keep you from scoring! Why not let one team do their thing for the first quarter; and then let the other team have their turn? Why all that knocking and blocking, tackling and resisting? But then, who'd really play golf on the course I have described. What would you pay to watch a football game such as the one I've described?

I did my first (and only) marathon a few years ago. That's 26.2 miles! It took me just over four hours to complete! And there is no way I could have finished except that I tackled the obstacles of sore muscles, rain, sleet and snow conditions on those many training runs, getting ready for that marathon. Adversity and obstacles helped prepare me for the victory I sought; that of crossing that finish line, thus doing what only about one percent of the entire population in America has ever done. It's the persimmon secret all over again!

To learn to handle victory, you must first learn to handle defeat! A veteran is "one who has been through it." He's learned by experience and determination to handle it! A child goes off to college and comes back a grown man or woman. He had no one to push him to study. No one to tell him when to go to bed or get up in the morning. No one to tell him how to act. It is coping with these "hard knocks" that mature and develop the child into a grown, qualified person.

I spent four years in the United States Air Force. I shouldered little responsibility at home. I never made up my bed. I soon found out my sargeant wasn't going to do it for me. And then they sent me overseas to Korea. There were further brutal lessons about life. But without these adversities, I'm sure I wouldn't have gained maturity. No freeze, no sweetness! No adversity, no maturity!

Do you want to help someone who is going through some tragedy? Who do you send? Someone who knows how it feels, someone who has been through it and survived, right? That's the persimmon secret. So around our church, I can send Walt Erwin or Glenda Crawford. They'll do a beautiful job helping that person to cope and conquer. Why can't I, a minister of the gospel, do as well? No pain, no sweetness! I haven't been there. I don't know what to say to a person going through it . Similarly, anyone going through divorce, cancer or death of a loved one, I'll do what I can. But the best I can do is send someone who has gone through the "freeze" and has thawed to sweetness!

The Bible says, "Suffering produces perseverance" (Rom. 5:3). Again, "...perseverance must finish its work so that you may be mature and complete, not lacking anything" (James 1:2). Sounds like the persimmon again, doesn't it!?

Someone has said, "Life is a grindstone. Whether it polishes you up or grinds you down depends on the stuff of which you are made!" You see lots of older people! Some are sweet, and some are crotchety! What's the difference? Was it that some faced hard times and others didn't? More likely it is the *way* they chose to handle adversity. Age alone doesn't do it. Around our church, there are older people who are cynical and sour; others are happy, radiant and positive. The difference is in the story of the persimmon. The freeze makes persimmons sweet! The same freeze makes other fruits bitter and sour! So with people!

Shall we pray to the Father, "Deliver us from problems, adversity, obstacles, tragedies and crises!"? No! Let's pray for wisdom and strength to handle these things as they mold us into something sweet, gentle and worthwhile!

So fate has thrown you a curve! Some batters strike out because of the curve. Others hit home runs! Just look around you in life. Folks pretty clearly have settled into "sweet" and "sour." You can easily distinguish them. And now you know it isn't a matter of fate or luck. It is a choice! A choice about what you do with adversity!

It is not within our power to "have" or "not have" adversity. At one time or another, in one way or another, problems "freezes," will come to all. Your only choice is what you do about them. Remember the persimmon. You can become as sweet as a persimmon which has survived the freeze...or you can become "sour grapes!" The choice is yours!

CHAPTER 22

"WHO WROTE THE BOOK ON NORMAL?"

ARE you normal? Many people in America are dissatisfied with themselves. They don't feel they "measure up." And my question is "TO WHAT?"! Who wrote the standard by which we measure ourselves? What has caused this great fear so many people have that they are not quite "normal"? That elusive standard on "normal" has caused a widespread fear about ourselves. "I'm too fat" or "I'm too skinny"; "My hips are too big." "My bust is too small." " My feet are too long," "My eyes are too close together." Who wrote the standard on how high cheek bones are supposed to be? What *is* the proper, normal length for feet or the *standard* distance between the eyes?

A few years ago, Bruce Feirstein wrote a little book "Real Men Don't Eat Quiche!" He had a ball with it! The public was incensed. He appeared on the Phil Donahue show. The audience tried to eat him alive. Who gave him the right to say who "real men" were, anyway? Bruce was laughing all the way to the bank. "Real men" eat steak rare, wear jockey shorts, don't use purple combs, drive pickup trucks, play racketball, and don't play badminton," etc.! He gave names of real men and quiche eaters. It caused a furor. But that's precisely the point. He knew it would hit their emotions. He knew no one has the right to write the book on "normal." But we allow unseen, unknown authors to do it all the time. And we offer our lifestyles, and perhaps even our destinies, (certainly our pocketbooks) to these phantom writers on "normal."

Emily Post and Amy Vanderbilt have long told us what is proper decorum at social occasions. It reminds me of a wedding I performed in a small Oklahoma town a number of years back. There were more people in the wedding party, than there were in the audience. The rehearsal for this event was interrupted several times while the etiquette book was brought out to see just how each event was to run. And yet, "what *is* proper?" Who has the right to say? This wedding was done by the book! But are they more married than the couple who stands before me in my office for a few words, a kiss and I send them on their way? Will marriages "done by the book" last longer than the informal kind?

Now please understand, I'm not opposed to doing things formal; even "according to the book." But do it because you "choose" to do it; not because you *must*!

A few years back we had a saying, "blue and green should never be seen." And to my mind, no one would have been caught dead in blue pants and a green shirt (or perhaps green skirt and blue sweater). But today those colors are among the most popular in anything from clothes to curtains; from carpet to wall paper. Now it's nice to be in fashion; just don't let the "authors on normal" completely run your life. Variety may be the spice of life, but it can also deplete your finances, keep you in frustration, just trying to stay fashionable. You can overdo this "normal" business. I see folks with fears, inhibitions, prejudices and insecurity, just trying to stay "normal." They have low self-esteem and stay unhappy and embarrassed. Someone's standards of "normal" have left them feeling abnormal or subnormal. Just who wrote the book on "normal"?

The Only Book That Counts

One book came with you when you were born. You've only got one "Owners Manual." You got one with your new car. You got an owners' manual with most everything you've ever bought, from cameras and computers to appliances and lawn mowers. These owner's manuals are not to inhibit you but to help you. The maker knows all about the product. They want you, the buyer, to understand it and get full benefit from it. So they write a book. And it's like a sign I saw once on a complicatd computer, "When all else fails, read instructions."

The Bible is like that. It was written by God, Who designed you and the world you live in. He knows all about it. He understands every principle of life. He gave you every feeling and desire you have. And His Book, your owner's manual, is to help you understand what it's all about and give you maximum pleasure and benefits! Let's look at a few pages!

First of all, we read that God created us "male and female"! So if you are either of these, you qualify as "normal"! It was later said that "Whosoever believes in Him shall have everlasting life" (John 3:16). Now if you come under the term "whosoever," you still qualify as "normal"! Your Owner's Manual further states that God gave man *dominion* over all He created (Gen. 1:28). That means that man can fly as high as he can dream. He has the right to go to the limits of the universe if he can get there. Some Christians have wondered whether man has any right to be flying off to the moon or other places in space. This verse gives us the right to go anywhere in God's universe. Now that authority was given to "man" (meaning "mankind"). If you are included in this term, you are "normal." That's good news, isn't it!? God further said, "I set before you life and death...now choose life" (Deut. 30:11-20). The rights of success, life, happiness, health, prosperity and eternal life, are before us...all of us. We are all in the same class. That means we are all "normal"!

I look in God's Book on Normal for "superior" and "inferior." I don't find where He created some to be superior and others inferior. The Bible doesn't divide us into smart and dumb; into treasure and trash. Just who is it the Lord loves, prefers, accepts and saves? Is it color, race, IQ, prosperity or accomplishment? Good news! It isn't either! "All" are invited (Matt. 11:28-30); God's great commission is to everyone. "Go into all the world, and preach the gospel to every creature" (Mark 16:15). And the Bible further explains, "There is neither Jew nor Greek, slave nor free, male nor female, for you are all one in Christ Jesus" (Gal. 3:28).

One of the best pieces of scripture on this is found in the second chapter of James. A fellow comes into one of our church meetings dressed "fit to kill." He has on a five hundred dollar suit, Rolex watch, and alligator shoes. Another fellow comes in wearing clothes from Goodwill Industries. Nothing matches, and he hasn't bathed in a week. If we show partiality to the rich man over the poor man, we "sin." Pretty plain, isn't it! And you know why? Because God judges the heart. Now maybe we should all look our best and try to dress appropriately at all occasions, but we are all "normal." Churches, above all other groups must realize this and deal with all men as sons and daughters of the King! God is "color blind" and Heaven is a "mixed Neighborhood"!

One last slice from the Book on "Normal." It is from First Corinthians, chapter twelve. From verses twelve to twenty-six, we are told the church is like a human body. We are all parts, each different from the other, but all needed and all necessary. Some are "eyes, feet, ears, noses." Some parts are more noticeable. Some seem more important. But scripture insists that all are needed, and that it would be a catastrophe if we were all alike. The verse I like best (v. 18) says, "But in fact God has arranged the parts in the body, every one of them, just as He wanted them to be!"

Just so in life some are extroverts and some are introverts.

Some are "crowd people" and some are "loners." Some are highly educated, some don't have any formal education at all. These differences are unimportant. Who wrote the book on "normal"?

So enjoy the way God made you. Do your best with what you have and are! Share with others. Love the Lord. Accept yourself as He accepts you! For we finally discovered who wrote the book on normal and guess what? You're normal!

CHAPTER 23

LOOKING AT LIFE THROUGH PROPER PERSPECTACLES!

"Dear Mom:

Sorry I haven't written sooner. My arm really has been broken. I broke it, and my left leg, when I jumped from the second floor of my dormitory...when we had the fire. We were lucky. A young service station attendant saw the blaze and called the Fire Department. They were there in minutes. I was in the hospital for a few days. Paul, the service station attendant, came to see me every day. And because it was taking so long to get our dormitory liveable again, I moved in with him. He has been so nice.

I must admit that I am pregnant, and I have a funny rash that the doctors call a "social disease." But don't worry, Mom, the shots are working, and we have an abortion clinic nearby.

Paul and I plan to get married just as soon as he can get a divorce.

I hope things are fine at home. I'm doing fine, and will write more when I get the chance.
Love,

Your daughter,
Susie

P.S. None of the above is true. But I did get a "C" in Sociology and flunked Chemistry. I just wanted you to receive this news in its "proper perspective!"

I heard Dr. James Dobson give a letter similar to this in one his speeches on the home. Everything is "compared to what?" Many things depend on your perspective! It was certainly true in this case.

Now of course you can overdo this business of "looking on the bright side." One fellow was incurable with his, "it could have been worse." A man fell from the twelfth floor. He was lying on the pavement when this fellow walked by. "It could have been worse," he proclaimed to an onlooker. "Just how could it have been worse than this? He fell to his death!" "Well," he said, "He could have fallen *on* someone!" Small comfort!

There are thousands of "mother-in-law" jokes. One involved the definition of "mixed feelings." It was described as watching your mother-in-law drive over the cliff in *your* new sports car!

But really, everything is relative! One fellow was asked, "How's your wife?" To which he replied, "Compared to what?"

There's a good "perspective" story in the Bible in Second Kings, chapter six. The King of Aram was at war with Israel. The only trouble was that Israel knew Aram's every move. Every ambush was thwarted and their army put to flight. The King was furious. He figured he had a spy for Israel among his ranks. But he was told, "We are all loyal to the King. The problem lies in Israel. They have a prophet named Elisha. Everything the King says in his bedroom, Elisha knows and informs Israel to beware." So plans were made to kill Elisha in Dothan where he was camped out with a servant.

The scene would fit into a good movie. Early in the morning Elisha's servant came out to do the chores. He stretched his arms and looked around. To his horror, he saw the army of Aram completely surrounding their campsite. Just Elisha and He against a countless horde. He wrung his hands, and wailed to Elisha, "Oh, what shall we do, my Lord? We're surrounded, and they're going to kill us!" Elisha comforted him with the words, "They that are with us are more than they that are with them." And then Elisha prayed to God. "Lord, open his eyes." And the Lord opened the servant's eyes, and behold, the mountains and skies were full of the army of God. It was the army of Aram in the minority. It all depends on your perspective.

Perspective! It keeps us from "majoring in minors." It keeps our attention on the things that are really important. It keeps us from worrying needlessly about trivials. Your son tore the seat out of his new blue jeans. Your husband leaves his dirty clothes on the bedroom floor, and "I have to pick them up!" Of course, you don't have to pick them up if you don't want to. There are lots of alternatives. You can nail them to the floor. You can burn them in the incinerator; you can mail them to China. You might even ask him nicely (for the hundredth time) to please put them in the dirty clothes hamper. Or you can simply remind yourself that he is a warm and loving man who is faithful to you. You can continue picking up those clothes if these things are more important to you than a couple of socks in the middle of the room.

"These kids dirty up the house," you say! But one day they'll be gone. And perhaps in that big, quiet, lonely house, you might wish it was dirty once again; and that the noise and clatter that once drove you crazy again made music in your heart.

"She squeezes the toothpaste in the middle!" "They never say 'thank you'; I'll never do it for them again!"

We need to see the "Big Picture"! We need to learn to distinguish between the essential and the insignificant. Will it matter five hundred years from now? Maybe it's not all that significant. Maybe I shouldn't get so stirred up about it. What *really is* important? Lift yourself up, and take a clear look at life through "proper perspectacles"!

THE "TWO LIST" CONCEPT!

Elsewhere in this book and in "You Can't Fly to Heaven in a Straight Line" (written a few years back), and in just about every speech I give, I mention that everyone has "two lists"! You have "Reasons to be happy," and "Reasons to be sad." We all have both lists. Just think about it for a moment. Get out a blank piece of paper and see if you can't write some things in both columns. And it is your choice which of those lists you emphasize. There are so many good things going on in the world, and in your own life, it ill behooves any of us to be "accentuating the negative"!

I find I have just enough thorns to make me appreciate roses; just enough critics to keep me from becoming arrogant. Just enough obstacles to keep me trying for success. Just enough failures to keep me leaning on God. Just enough heartache to make me appreciate celebration; and just enough love, joy and success to keep me *DELIRIOUS!*

Well, then, where can you get "perspectacles" to help you see the things about which I've spoken? First of all, you've got eyes. You've got to "open them"! Elisha prayed, "Lord, open his eyes." You can't see anything with your eyes closed. Someone has said, "No one is so blind as he who will not see!"

Again, the Bible admonished, "Lift *up* your eyes!" You've got to get your eyes off the ground; off your shoes. Lots of folks have the "downward look." All they ever see are the cracks in the sidewalk; the gloom and doom in the world. You have to look up to see the blue sky, the birds, the lovely mountains and the sunrise. You have to look up to see opportunity, privilege and blessing. There's plenty of exciting things to see for the one who will "lift up his eyes."

And lastly, I think it important to look into the Word if you would really see clearly. The Bible says, "Open my eyes, that I may see wonderful things out of Your law" (Ps. 119:18). God designed this Universe. He thought you up!

He loves you and knows what's best. He wrote His Book to show you how to get zest and gusto from life. There is excitement and thrills for the one who puts on "proper perspectacles" and sees the glory of NOW, and the VICTORY of Eternity!

CHAPTER 24

SEEDS COME BEFORE FLOWERS!

A seed packet bore the inscription, "The flowers of your tomorrow are in the seeds of today!" That has a lot more meaning in it than just the seeds in that little package. And isn't it a strange contrast; that picture on the label, and those seeds inside? It is nearly always true that flowers are prettier than their seeds. And some of the most beautiful flowers in the world come from seeds that are so ugly it is almost unbelievable.

No one would ever think of shopping for seeds, without knowing what they will become. A seed store without pictures of the outcome would not sell much. But that's what you start with, seeds!

There is a basic law of "cause and effect!" That's another way of stating, "seeds come before flowers!" We will discuss the laws of sowing and reaping a little later on. Right now we want to impress you with this one law. We are always wanting to violate it. We want to eat junk food, yet become healthy and fit! We want to sow neglect and reap attention; sleep around, yet marry a virgin! We want to throw money away, yet become rich! We seek a good marriage while abusing or neglecting our mates and kids. We live like the devil and want the reward of an angel! But the abuse of today will destroy our tomorrow! Said another way, "the wrinkles of tomorrow are in the frowns of today!"

Where we are today is the result of what we planted yesterday! You may say, "I didn't ask my mate to leave me"; "I didn't plan on my kids getting hung up on drugs," or "I surely didn't want that car to run over me." But what you did (or do) about it is more important! Our past explains us, but it doesn't lock us in. "As the twig is bent, the tree will grow." And we are the sum total of all the decisions we've made. Look at your past. Your past training and experiences, good and bad! Your past attitude! What seeds have you planted before today?

Now what lies ahead in your future depends on the seeds you are planting today! You are in charge of your destiny, and you plant seeds every day you live. And it will all catch up with us someday. Paper mills understand this law and they plant trees they won't cut for a hundred years. Two birds flying by, observed a worm climbing an apple tree in the dead of winter. "Silly worm," they exclaimed, "There's no apples in that tree!" But the wise worm replied, "There will be when I get there!"

We program our own future. A man ran a very successful restaurant! His son was an economics major in college. On one of his trips home, the son explained to his father that they predicted a recession ahead, and his father should get ready for it. He should not repaint this year. He suggested cutting back on the portions of food served, shop for cheaper prices in meat, lay off a couple of waitresses. In this way, he said, his dad would be ready for the recession. Well, the recession came. And his dad was so glad his son had warned him. What he couldn't understand was that the restaurant across the street was doing more business than ever! You see we make our recessions! One optimist was asked, "What are you going to do about the depression?" His quick reply, "I'm not going to participate!"

So it seems pretty important to plant the right seeds today for the flowers of tomorrow. Financially, you must save, invest, and insure for tomorrow's retirement. Physically, you must eat right, exercise and get enough rest. Your attitude today must be positive to insure tomorrow's fitness. In marriage lots of seed planting must be done so that when the kids are grown and gone, and it's "just the two of us again," it can be bliss and not blah! And if you want a beautiful Eternity you must learn "you can't live like Hell and spend Eternity in Heaven!" You can have anything you want. But don't forget, "seeds come first"!

There's a verse in the Bible, really a *LAW*! It goes like this. "Do not be deceived. God cannot be mocked. A man reaps what he sows" (Gal. 6:7). From this I want to discuss six laws of sowing and reaping. Notice I said "Laws," not theories or possibilities. Laws! Absolutes! And here they are.

First, you must sow to reap! We all know folks standing on the pier of life waiting for their ship to come in. But we all know they haven't sent one *out*! If hoping, wishing or even talking would bring the flowers, we'd all have them. But until you put seeds in the ground, it does little good to dream of flowers. They will stay just that...dreams!

Secondly, you will reap what you sow! Sunflower seeds produce sunflowers. Corn produces corn. And in life we are going to get back precisely what we have sown! Now this puts total control in our own hands. For if we can decide which seeds to plant, we can determine which flowers will grow in our garden. And it works both ways, good or bad. If you want trouble, sow it. You'll get plenty of it back! But if you want friends, love and success, you've got to sow these things to get them back in your life.

Thirdly, you will reap in a different season than you sow! Every farmer knows this. The rest of us should become acquainted with this law too. We get so impatient. We want to throw an egg in the barnyard tonight and hear it crow in the morning. I heard of a sign on the highway, "Antiques Manufactured While You Wait." It takes time for seed to become flowers. And don't go out there and dig up the seeds to see if they are growing. That's our problem in life. We dig it up too soon. We give up and abandon perfectly good plans when all we need is a little patience.

Fourthly, you reap more than you sow! One kernal of corn planted becomes a stalk. And on that stalk grow many ears of corn. And on each ear, hundreds of little kernals! And isn't it encouraging in life to know that what you do, will come back to you in multiplied measure. Pressed down, shaken together and running over, will be poured into your lap. "For with the measure you use, it will be measured to you" (Luke 6:38). Marvelous verse! Great reassurance to those of us who really want to reap abundantly.

And fifthly, you will reap in direct proportion to what you sow! This is principle number four carried further. Not only does it work with the one seed, but if you keep planting it starts an avalanche effect. Again drawing from the best book on "Seeds and Flowers," "whoever sows generously, will also reap generously" (2 Cor. 9:6). Any good salesperson knows that if you just stay out there, doing what you're supposed to do, in a polite and positive manner, the benefits will come in. At first they will trickle in. And then it becomes a steady stream; and finally an avalanche!

And principle number six is the clincher! *You cannot change yesterday's yield, but you can determine tomorrow's harvest!* We may have a lot of regrets about yesterday. But the important thing is what are you going to do about it? In farming, you can plow up, fertilize and replant the soil, and tomorrow's harvest will be different. That's the encouraging part about life. What has happened to you is not as important as what you do about it! The number of your problems, or even the size of your problems isn't the important thing. It's what you do about your problems that makes some people rise to the top of the ladder of success. Others may sink to the bottom. It's all determined by this last principle. So you made mistakes in the past. Did you learn anything? What do you want to happen today, and more importantly, tomorrow? You cannot change yesterday's yield; but you can determine tomorrow's harvest!

The story is told of two men who died and went to heaven. One had been rich on earth, but deeply involved in self interests alone. The other had been poor, but rich in helping others. Saint Peter showed them to their houses. The poor man was shown to a house that was fabulous beyond his wildest dreams. The rich man thought, "Boy, if his looks like that, mine must be a castle indeed!" But he was disappointed to see that his own house was a most modest cottage. Saint Peter explained, "We could only build with the materials you sent on ahead!"

Truly in life, and in Eternity, "The Flowers of Your Tomorrow Are in the Seeds of Your Today!"

CHAPTER 25

QUALITY CONTROL!

I'M down now to the final chapter in this book! And the feeling consumes me, "Have I told you anything really important?" Have I said these things with sufficient power to get your attention, to change the course and destiny of your life? Has it been worth your while to read this book?

I must talk about quality! Quality of life! Quality, as opposed to quantity! Meaning as well as longevity! It's all very well to speak of adding years to your life. But I'm more concerned with adding "life" to your years!

And we're all familiar with quality control. Some of you work as "quality control inspectors." In this age of mass production, we've come to realize that if we don't produce quality, the number of items completed is worthless. If our clothes shrink at first washing, what good was it to set records in the number of such articles produced in a given day? If the brakes fail on our automobiles, would price and numbers mean anything? Quantity is important; but only as long as we retain quality!

Yet we're geared to think of life in terms of quantity! We want to live as long as we can. So we do lots of research. We take numerous vitamins. We have all kinds of health food fads and diets. All this to add a few more precious years to this life.

Remember the days of Carter's Little Liver Pills? One guy

faithfully took one of these every day of his life. He died at the ripe old age of one hundred three. It is said that they had to take a stick and beat his liver to death! I don't think we can verify the truth of that story. But some of us remember the days of Hadacol with all its testimonies for long life and good health. It has given way to Geritol, and numerous others. We're all in this quest for quantity...longevity!

But quantity doesn't solve life's pressures and problems. Shakespeare had his "seven stages of life." From birth to school age, we are basically selfish. It is "Me first" and "I want it now!" From grade one to the teen years, we are learning, competing, feeling awkward, and learning team effort and cooperation.

In the teen years it is wonderful beyond belief. Right? Wrong! The teens hit you with peer pressure. Whether you are "with it" or a "nerd" depends on so many things. And it affects the way you dress, how you fix your hair and the kind of music to which you listen. You develop a whole new vocabulary, so that your parents don't have any idea what you are talking about. This is the age of dating. It is dangerous, perilous, delirious and marvelous, all at the same time. It is a time of "becoming"!

Marriage sends you into a new dimension of "relationships." Now it is "us" and "we," and everything you do affects the other person. You are trying to get your heads above water financially. There are decisions to be made all the time. And every one of them seems a matter of life or death.

And then you hit "midlife," and for many, this is a crisis! Senior, but not senile! Followed by old age and "life is a mist" and before you know it, it is gone!

How long you live is important. But more important, by far, is how well you've lived. How happy have you been? How content? How really successful? And quality is what you begin to search for. Midlife hits like an atomic bomb.

For some it is a glorious "shifting of gears." For others

it is the "beginning of the end!" There are rumblings from within. What will I do with the rest of my life? The years bring change! There is change of jobs, change of location; and for some, a change of mates! Thoughts turn to the matter of health and fitness; and then to the spiritual. Is there really a God? What is my purpose in being on this earth? What lies beyond the grave?

Many go a little crazy at mid-life! They change their appearance. They make a last ditch effort to be young again; to get what they feel they've missed out on. They may buy a new sports car; or get a mistress. One guy got a mistress who had a new sports car!

But it's a great time to re-assess life's values. If this is done carefully, wisely and prayerfully, this is a wonderful idea. But if we're going to become concerned with "quality control," there are some guidelines that will help. I suggest six!

Come to terms with yourself! It is time to quit warring with yourself. Maybe you've been competing with others unnecessarily. Perhaps you should stop trying to be something (someone) you're not. Accept your origin, your potential and your self worth. Accept your mission and your destiny. You have the freedom to become whatever you choose to become. Choose wisely! But choose boldly and confidently!

Set quality goals! Set goals for your health, wealth, travel, service to others, and relationships. Think about these carefully. Make them specific, and set them down on paper! Do something every day toward these goals!

Get out of "yourself"! Don't take yourself too seriously. Lots of people and projects need your help. The best way to deal with self pity and worry is to be concerned with others. Take an interest in your neighborhood, your country, your fellow man, and your church!

Get a "valve job" on your "laughter mechanism"! Develop a sense of humor. This is so important in coping with stress. Laughter is a valve. Our lives are like balloons. They are made for pressure; just not too much of it. And if you pump too much into them, they explode...balloons... *and* lives! Learn to see the bright side. Learn to laugh! Laughter is a "choice," you know. Anyone can laugh; anytime you choose! And there are so many things to laugh about. Just look in the mirror! See what I mean? See a "Pink Panther" movie. Enjoy a good joke. Laugh with friends. Learn to laugh at yourself. Laughter will add length and quality to your life.

Value the "journey" as well as the destination! There's an old hymn we sing in church. It's called "In the Sweet By and By"! It's a grand old song, but there's also the "Sweet Here and Now"! See the end of life as the best. At fifty-three more than half my life is gone. Which half is the best? If I live to be 80 (and I plan to live much longer than that), which forty would be the best years? The first, with the teen years, dating, marriage, birth of our own children? Or the last forty, with love growing deeper, more peace and serenity, seeing the children marry well, grandbabies, and depth...with a greater sense of Eternity? The last half is the best, "hands down." But only if you've paid attention to "quality control." I saw a greeting card recently. It said simply, "Come along, grow old with me...the best is yet to be!" Ah , so true!

And lastly, most importantly, *come to terms with God*! Perhaps you came through a period of doubt and skepticism. Maybe there was a time when you thought you knew best. So you ran after all kinds of materialistic goals, only to find they did not satisfy. Now you're ready to restudy the fact that you've been made in the Image of God. You have an inherent spiritual hunger. And just like the physical hunger you experience, it can only be satisfied with the right things. God says, "Try me and see" (Mal. 3:10, 11). All those who have done so have found Him satisfying and His way best. Jesus said, "I came that you might have life, and have it to the full" (John 10:10). You find in God, that you never need to be alone; now or in Eternity.

So whatever trophies you accumulate on this earth, you

will find that quantity is fine, but quality is better! And Heaven is going to be better than you've dreamed! See you there?